Come...
Getting Acquainted
with the
Godhead

TEDI H. MARSHALL

My Prayer, Inc.
Chicago, IL USA

Come...Getting Acquainted with the Godhead
by Tedi H. Marshall

First Printing – October 2013
ISBN: 978-1-60047-918-2
Contact Tedi Marshall by email: marshall.tedi@gmail.com
Library of Congress Control Number: 2013952372

Unless otherwise noted, all Scripture is from
the King James Version of the Bible.

References to satan and related names in this writing
are not capitalized. I choose not to give him
any reverent acknowledgment.

Printed in the U.S.A.

0   1   2   3   4   5   6   7   8   9   10   11   12   13   14

This book is dedicated to the Godhead...Father, Son and Holy Spirit. He is the Head of my life; my I AM. Thank You, Lord God for the honor and privilege of representing You in service and in these pages. Glory to Your holy Name!

ACKNOWLEDGEMENTS

Thank you to my parents, Johnny *(has gone to be with the Lord)* and Theodora Hartman, who instilled what I did not understand at the time – integrity and values; with a little extra special for my mother, a great woman of God, who continues to exude love, wisdom and encouragement; to my sons, Brandyn and Joseph, mighty men of valor, who know just when to call and how to respectfully say it "straight with no chaser" when they do; and to my sister, Lori Hartman, who has the knack of giving that sometimes annoying but much needed push, always encouraging.

Thank you to the greats who have paved the way for me in teaching the full Gospel of truth and imparting so freely what the Lord has given them, my Pastor, William S. Winston, Daryl L. Barnett, Kenneth and Gloria Copeland, Creflo Dollar, John Eckhardt, Michael D. Reynolds, Vincent C. Lambert, Kenneth E. Hagin, Victor Torres, Randy Gilbert, and so many other teachers of workshops, seminars, conferences and writings.

Thank you to the support system the Lord assigned, Ann Pinkney, Michelle Collins Leaks, John Pinkney; and special appreciation to Sandra Brown *(too much to list it all)*, Saundra Wright and Gwen Pinkney who also reviewed and edited the manuscript, and Kyra Johnson, who also assisted with the cover concept.

Thank you to all who answered the Lord's call to pray, answer questions, encourage, give a hug and support. I pray a special blessing for you all...in Jesus' Name. Amen.

PREFACE

John 15:3-11

[3] Now ye are clean through the word which I have spoken unto you.

[4] Abide in Me, and I in you. As the branch cannot bear fruit of itself, except it abide in the vine; no more can ye, except ye abide in Me.

[5] I am the Vine, ye *are* the branches: He that abideth in Me, and I in him, the same bringeth forth much fruit: for without Me ye can do nothing.

[6] If a man abide not in Me, he is cast forth as a branch, and is withered; and men gather them, and cast *them* into the fire, and they are burned.

[7] If ye abide in Me, and My words abide in you, ye shall ask what ye will, and it shall be done unto you.

[8] Herein is my Father glorified, that ye bear much fruit; so shall ye be My disciples.

[9] As the Father hath loved Me, so have I loved you: continue ye in My love.

[10] If ye keep My commandments, ye shall abide in My love; even as I have kept My Father's commandments, and abide in His love.

[11] These things have I spoken unto you, that My joy might remain in you, and *that* your joy might be full.

God lets us know the fruit bearing is in the connection with the vine. In regard to our life as New Creatures by Jesus Christ, it is not just any connection, but a connection of intimacy...the up close and personal with the Lord. This fruit is not merely of things, programs and promotions. Kingdom fruit encompasses so much more – peace that passes all understanding; unspeakable joy; is where joy equates to strength...strength to stand tall, conquer, persevere, and praise His Name regardless – in times of little and times of much. It is within this profound connection that we worship the Lord; from the innermost part of our being – to bless Him with all that is within us. Hallelujah!

Whether you are just approaching a life in Christ, have been a believer for years or are somewhere in-between there is always more to know and a deeper place to inhabit in Him. We grow from glory to glory and revelation to revelation in God. He is alive and revealing more of Himself to us all the time. As He has completed His work of love through Jesus Christ so we may know Him, it becomes our responsibility to accept His invitation to do so.

This book will lead and introduce you to the Godhead: Father, Son and Holy Spirit; but you must decide to abide; to join Him in intimacy; to delve into oneness with Him; desiring Him as He desires you. If you do, I promise your life will never be the same.

So now, *COME*...get acquainted with the Godhead. He awaits you.

Amen.

TABLE OF CONTENTS

INTRODUCTION

The Lord God has established many benefits for us at becoming one of His own by Salvation through Jesus Christ. These are all wonderful – He withholds no good thing from us. However, there is that part that must never be overlooked or taken for granted...the Godhead, that is, God Himself.

One of the greatest benefits we have in Salvation – having accepted and confessed Jesus Christ as personal Lord and Savior – is the ability to fellowship with God. Now God, in His great love and affection – He cannot help it, it is who He is...Love – has set things in order so we can enjoy intimacy with Him. This is to walk with Him, talk with Him as a dear Friend...yes, just as Enoch, we can also.

This by no means indicates that we are to disregard any reverence for the Lord...He is God, and there in none higher. Hallowed is His Name, to be regarded as holy. To be able to regard Him in the manner due Him as well as become as close in fellowship as Enoch, we must become acquainted with Him; to learn about Him, His likes and dislikes; to learn His nature and characteristics, which is to learn His Name.

The objective for this writing is to introduce the Godhead, so you may begin your journey of intimacy with the One who loves you so dearly, that He gave of Himself so you could have life and have it more abundantly. Amen.

Ephesians 1:17-19 *Amplified Bible*
[17] [For I always pray to] the God of the Lord Jesus Christ, the Father of glory, that He my grant you a spirit of wisdom and revelation [of insight into mysteries and secrets] in the [deep and intimate] knowledge of Him,

[18] By having the eyes of your heart flooded with light, so that you can know and understand the hope to which He has called you, and how rich is His glorious inheritance in the saints (His set-apart ones),

[19] And [so that you can know and understand] what is the immeasurable and unlimited and surpassing greatness of His power in and for us who believe, as demonstrated in the working of His mighty strength

It is God's desire and intent for us to know Him, understand His ways, and live worthily – not as in "worthy" vs. "unworthy," as though the Blood of Jesus is of none or limited effect; but worthy as in walking according to who He is and who we are in Him. We are to live and operate as New Creatures in Christ – walking, talking, living testimonies of what He can and will do for those who turn to Him. It all begins with becoming acquainted with the One to whom we are to turn, the Godhead.

THE GODHEAD

<u>FOUNDATION SCRIPTURES</u>:
John 1:1
In the beginning was the Word, and the Word was with God, and the Word was God.

John 10:30
I and My Father are One.

Romans 1:20
For the invisible things of Him from the creation of the world are clearly seen, being understood by the things that are made, even His eternal power and Godhead; so that they are without excuse

1 John 5:7
For there are three that bear record in heaven, the Father, the Word, and the Holy Ghost: and these three are One.

The Godhead consists of all three persons of God – the Lord, our heavenly Father; Jesus Christ, who is the Son of God and our Lord and Savior; and Holy Spirit (Holy Ghost), who is the Spirit of God, our Comforter, Teacher and Helper, sent to us as promised. All three, the completeness of who and all God is – Father, Son and Holy Spirit – were there in the beginning of human history.

And God said, Let <u>us</u> make man in <u>our</u> image, after <u>our</u> likeness... Genesis 1:26a

Acts 17:22-30

[22] Then Paul stood in the midst of Mars' hill, and said, Ye men of Athens, I perceive that in all things ye are too superstitious.

[23] For as I passed by, and beheld your devotions, I found an altar with this inscription, TO THE UNKNOWN GOD. Whom therefore ye ignorantly worship, Him declare I unto you.

[24] God that made the world and all things therein, seeing that He is Lord of heaven and earth, dwelleth not in temples made with hands;

[25] Neither is worshipped with men's hands, as though He needed any thing, seeing He giveth to all life, and breath, and all things;

[26] And hath made of one blood all nations of men for to dwell on all the face of the earth, and hath determined the times before appointed, and the bounds of their habitation;

[27] That they should seek the Lord, if haply they might feel after Him, and find Him, though He be not far from every one of us:

[28] For in Him we live, and move, and have our being; as certain also of your own poets have said, For we are also His offspring.

[29] Forasmuch then as we are the offspring of God, we ought not to think that the Godhead is like unto gold, or silver, or stone, graven by art and man's device.

[30] And the times of this ignorance God winked at; but now commandeth all men every where to repent

The time for man's worshiping God by rote – impersonal and limited to ceremony – ceased with the death, burial, resurrection and ascension of Jesus Christ. Everything that separated us from God by the act of treason perpetrated by Adam in the Garden of Eden is removed by the great sacrifice of love through Jesus Christ.

The ability and opportunity to come into relationship with God and progressing on to fellowship with Him is restored.   The Lord's desire was always for us to fellowship, worship and commune with Him; and to ensure that we can and do, He sent of Himself, of the Godhead in two ways:

- His Son, Jesus Christ – in the flesh, that we would be saved…the way to enter into a relationship with God

- His Spirit, Holy Ghost – in the spirit, to comfort, help, correct, teach and guide us into all truth

We will delve further into the characteristics, nature and functions in the Sections following.

John 4:24
God is a Spirit: and they that worship Him must worship Him in spirit and in truth.

We are created to worship God, to praise and magnify Him, but we are to do so in spirit and in truth; not just in "lip service," vain repetition in prayer or with chants, nor with mere religious or traditional ceremonies.   Real, true worship is from the heart…of the abundance there…the abundance of who God is and of His love.   We can do this because He first loved us.   So we can actually say that He set for us the standard for love and loving.

Luke 6:45
A good man out of the good treasure of his heart bringeth forth that which is good; and an evil man out of the evil treasure of his heart bringeth forth that which is evil: for of the abundance of the heart his mouth speaketh.

Psalm 34:3
O magnify the LORD with me, and let us exalt His Name together.

The best way to worship and praise the Lord in spirit and truth is to know Him, the One you are setting as your object *(Person)* of affection. As you become acquainted with the Godhead your heart becomes increasingly full of the knowledge, understanding and wisdom of God; it becomes complete and overflows with the accolades due only to Him. This is how you magnify the Lord; to make Him bigger than all else in your life; and He becomes the focus.

He desires to become real and alive in your heart; to overtake, renew and elevate you to the place "niched," carved out by Him, which can only be filled by a connection with Him. Look at it as your "spot" in Him, and His "spot" in you. He desires for you to become more than familiar with Him...to actually become One with Him.

The entire transformation begins with becoming acquainted with all three Persons of the Godhead. Only then will you learn to trust Him wholeheartedly...even when things appear grim, when the wait is long, and storms come, your very being will say, "Regardless of how it looks or how I feel, I know my God; He is still on the throne. He loves me and will deliver, produce or fulfill exactly what He said; all I need."

When you know the Godhead intimately you will no longer judge or limit Him based on your experiences with man, for you will know from your heart that:

- He is real, true and alive
- His promises are yea *(yes)* and amen *(so be it)*
- He is faithful
- He will never fail, leave, or forsake you

Then you can believe in, trust in, rely on, and be sold out to the One who gave His life for you.

Selah *(pause and seriously consider that)*

SECTION ONE

GETTING ACQUAINTED WITH JEHOVAH

FOUNDATION SCRIPTURE:
Exodus 3:14
And God said unto Moses, I AM THAT I AM: and He said,
Thus shalt thou say unto the children of Israel, I AM hath sent
me unto you.

INTRODUCTION
The first step in setting a firm foundation in your life in God
through Christ Jesus is in getting intimately acquainted with
Jehovah, the Father. Coming to know His goodness, faithfulness
and great love for you is the foundation for a victorious life; for
you will be enabled to continue standing while waiting for His
promises to come to pass and *especially* when opposition comes.

In intimacy with the Father, we are moved from intellectual
(head) knowledge of Him, to that up-close-and-personal *(heart)*
awareness and knowledge of Him. We gain an in depth
revelatory understanding of Him – Spirit to spirit, His to ours –

and in this, our faith is substantially built on a solid foundation. "Revelatory," as in He reveals the essence of Himself to us in response to our seeking and desiring to know Him.

As New Creatures in Christ, believing on the fumes of accounts passed on through the ages of a God spoken of by parents or grandparents, in happy songs sung as a child in Sunday school or day camp, in the hymns "Auntie" may have played, or images created by someone else's experience with the Lord are no longer substantial enough. They cannot satisfy the growing hunger and thirst, the strong desire to directly connect with our heavenly Father. We reach a point where we must **know** Him for ourselves; where we are walking with Him, conversing with Him, seeking Him, listening for Him; not making a move without Him.

As you may start out with, "Where are You, Lord," "Send me a sign Lord," – sincerely desiring to know and get close to Him – you will find, that a shift will occur as you learn more about Him. You will become One with Him. Moving *as* He moves. Speaking *as* He speaks. Going *with* Him…flowing *with* Him – as in a dance: two partners moving as one, with God having the lead.

In learning about Him, becoming acquainted, familiar with the Lord Jehovah:

- Your faith is established.
- Your confidence is established.
- Your strength is established.

All because a depth develops to your relationship *and* fellowship with Him.

CHAPTER I

JEHOVAH AS CREATOR

JEHOVAH AS CREATOR

Genesis 1:1-25

¹ In the beginning God created the heaven and the earth.

² And the earth was without form, and void; and darkness was upon the face of the deep. And the Spirit of God moved upon the face of the waters.

³ And God said, Let there be light: and there was light.

⁴ And God saw the light, that it was good: and God divided the light from the darkness.

⁵ And God called the light Day, and the darkness He called Night. And the evening and the morning were the first day.

⁶ And God said, Let there be a firmament in the midst of the waters, and let it divide the waters from the waters.

⁷ And God made the firmament, and divided the waters which were under the firmament from the waters which were above the firmament: and it was so.

⁸ And God called the firmament Heaven. And the evening and the morning were the second day.

⁹ And God said, Let the waters under the heaven be gathered together unto one place, and let the dry land appear: and it was so.

¹⁰ And God called the dry land Earth; and the gathering together of the waters called He Seas: and God saw that it was good.

¹¹ And God said, Let the earth bring forth grass, the herb yielding seed, and the fruit tree yielding fruit after his kind, whose seed is in itself, upon the earth: and it was so.

¹² And the earth brought forth grass, and herb yielding seed after his kind, and the tree yielding fruit, whose seed was in itself, after his kind: and God saw that it was good.

¹³ And the evening and the morning were the third day.

¹⁴ And God said, Let there be lights in the firmament of the heaven to divide the day from the night; and let them be for signs, and for seasons, and for days, and years:

¹⁵ And let them be for lights in the firmament of the heaven to give light upon the earth: and it was so.

¹⁶ And God made two great lights; the greater light to rule the day, and the lesser light to rule the night: He made the stars also.

¹⁷ And God set them in the firmament of the heaven to give light upon the earth,

¹⁸ And to rule over the day and over the night, and to divide the light from the darkness: and God saw that it was good.

¹⁹ And the evening and the morning were the fourth day.

²⁰ And God said, Let the waters bring forth abundantly the moving creature that hath life, and fowl that may fly above the earth in the open firmament of heaven.

²¹ And God created great whales, and every living creature that moveth, which the waters brought forth abundantly, after their kind, and every winged fowl after his kind: and God saw that it was good.

²² And God blessed them, saying, Be fruitful, and multiply, and fill the waters in the seas, and let fowl multiply in the earth.

²³ And the evening and the morning were the fifth day.

²⁴ And God said, Let the earth bring forth the living creature after his kind, cattle, and creeping thing, and beast of the earth after his kind: and it was so.

²⁵ And God made the beast of the earth after his kind, and cattle after their kind, and every thing that creepeth upon the earth after his kind: and God saw that it was good.

I have found that as I learn more about the Lord, spending more deliberate time with Him, I see His creations differently. *KNOWING* the Lord as CREATOR enables us to see the beauty in His handiwork; the intricate details as carved, painted, etched, sculpted, molded, fashioned by His hand, personally.

Consider nature:
The varieties of flowers – the vivid, vibrancy of colors and fragrances; even the intricate details in the trunk of a tree, which are like carvings; or the various hues in the different skies *(sunrise, sunset, seasonal, weather)*. These can oftentimes be missed in our comings and goings. The Holy Spirit is tapping you on the shoulder, telling you to pause and consider the works of the Lord.

Consider animals:
The uniqueness of animals, in their own beauty, is created with different elements for survival. Even bugs, as creepy as they may

seem to some, are intricate in appearance and distinct in the sounds they make. My youngest son was always interested in nature. Through his interest in animals I learned even more about the creative attribute of our God.

Consider mankind:

The process of reproduction and the body's ability to restore and replenish itself are truly amazing. Every person is a special, individual creation of the Lord Himself. Each of us has his/her own DNA *(deoxyribonucleic acid)* make up. Unfortunately, DNA is usually only considered in crime investigations; and we miss out on a great deal when we allow satan to dictate our view and perspective, setting limits. DNA takes on a whole new meaning when we look at it in the light of the LORD AS CREATOR.

- Your skin: made up of pores, follicles, cells, and melanin, which fashions the perfect skin tone just for you.

- Your fingerprints: no two people have the same fingerprints. The Lord took the time to etch perfect, exclusive fingerprints on each or your fingertips.

Yes, we have some characteristics from our parents, grandparents and so on, but there are things one person has that even a sibling will not have. Your sibling does not have the same exact make up of everything of your make up. Twins, as close as they are – can't get much closer than sharing a womb – and as much as one may feel the emotions of the other, are still individual works of the Lord God Almighty. There are so many things that make each of us a unique work of God. The things science may explain – cells, skin, hair, nails, flesh and bones – are all fashioned by God to house the real us, which is the **spirit man**.

Let's explore this further.

Genesis 1:26-28

²⁶ And God said, Let Us make man in Our image, after Our likeness: and let them have dominion over the fish of the sea, and over the fowl of the air, and over the cattle, and over all the earth, and over every creeping thing that creepeth upon the earth.

²⁷ So God created man in His own image, in the image of God created He him; male and female created He them.

²⁸ And God blessed them, and God said unto them, Be fruitful, and multiply, and replenish the earth, and subdue it: and have dominion over the fish of the sea, and over the fowl of the air, and over every living thing that moveth upon the earth.

Psalm 8:1, 3-6, 9 *Amplified Bible*

¹ O Lord, our Lord, how excellent (majestic and glorious) is Your name in all the earth! You have set Your glory on [or above] the heavens.

³ When I view *and* consider Your heavens, the work of Your fingers, the moon and the stars, which You have ordained *and* established,

⁴ What is man that You are mindful of him, and the son of [earthborn] man that You care for him?

⁵ Yet You have made him but a little lower than God [or heavenly beings], and You have crowned him with glory and honor.

⁶ You made him to have dominion over the works of Your hands; You have put all things under his feet:

⁹ O Lord, our Lord, how excellent (majestic and glorious) is Your name in all the earth!

As marvelous as our natural, physical bodies are, nothing beats the fact *and* truth that the "real us" is created in the likeness and image of God, who is Spirit. We are created in God's exact image – looking the same as He *(spirit)*; and in His likeness – operating as He operates *(with authority, having and taking dominion)*.

Yes, you have authority over the fish of the sea, birds of the air, over the cattle and every creeping thing that creeps on the earth. You have and are to operate in this authority now, in this time, <u>today</u>. Although Adam's act of high treason against God in the Garden of Eden moved mankind out of position of dominion, God's intent for us did not end there; He did not change His mind about our purpose – the purpose of mankind. It was already established, set before the foundation of the world.

Ancient myths portray mankind as an afterthought to carry out the drudgery work as slaves to the "gods," but **we are actually the pinnacle *(high-point, peak)* of God's creative works, crowned with glory**.

There is definite purpose to our existence; according to Genesis 1:26, 28, 2:15:

- To tend to, care for the creations/creatures of the one true God

- Participate in His creative work

- Act/operate as the Lord's representatives here on earth; multiplying, replenishing, subduing it

Isaiah 45:12
I have made the earth, and created man upon it: I, even My hands, have stretched out the heavens, and all their host have I commanded.

Let's consider Psalm 139:14
I will praise thee; for I am fearfully and wonderfully made: marvelous are thy works; and that my soul knoweth right well.

With God as Creator in mind and using Psalm 139:14 as your weapon of assurance against the devil, you can understand that you do <u>not</u> have to fall for *(believe)* satan's lies targeting your personal -esteem, -image and -confidence.

Instead, you can be sure that you are fearfully, wonderfully and awesomely made by God, His handiwork; and know right well in your soul that all His works, of which you are one, are MARVELOUS. You are to know this from the core of your being. Let it settle way down on the inside of you. When the devil comes with taunts of lowliness, inadequacy and failure, tell him, "In the Name of Jesus, get out of my camp. I am made in the magnificent image and likeness of God, and I am marvelous."

Jehovah God as Creator...awesome!

CHAPTER II

JEHOVAH AND HIS NAMES
(CHARACTERISTICS)

JEHOVAH AND HIS NAMES (CHARACTERISTICS)

There are various "Names" for Jehovah, God, which tell of His characteristics – distinctive, distinguishing qualities. In studying them, with the purpose of getting a better understanding of Who and All He is, and what He can and will do, we reinforce our foundation in Him and become more confident in Him, as we also discover what He is about. As a result we will depend on, rely on and trust in His capabilities and no longer just our own.

We know that He is God, and we pray to the One, True and Living God; however, in understanding His various characteristics we also gird up our faith in Him.

First things first:
In Luke chapter 11, the disciples asked the Lord, Jesus, to teach them to pray. His response is what is commonly referred to as "The Lord's Prayer." Verse 2, states the first line of that instructional prayer:

> Our Father which art in heaven, **Hallowed be thy name**…

Hallowed – to make or regard, honor as holy[1]; sanctify; consecrate, consider sacred, venerate[2]

Venerate – to hold in deep respect; revere; to honor in recognition of qualities of holiness, excellence, wisdom, etc.; worship[2]

In reviewing verse 2, based on these definitions, we can see that the Name of the Lord is...

- To be regarded as holy

- To be honored in recognition of qualities of holiness, excellence and wisdom

- To be praised and worshiped

Hebrews 6:13
For when God made promise to Abraham, because He could swear by no greater, He sware by Himself...

Genesis 22:16
By Myself have I sworn, saith the LORD...

There is no name higher than that of God. In making an oath to Abraham, God swore on His own Name because there is none higher.

A. WHAT IS IN A NAME?

The question has been asked: "What is in a name?"

Allow this example to answer that for you:
Have you ever been in a store or other crowd-type setting and a child cries out, "Mommy" or "Daddy"? Either several heads will turn or as with an older child's cry there may not be an instant reaction.

For the sake of this writing let's take into account an older child's call to a father: because of the generality of the name "Daddy," he may hear it, but not really; as it may not always immediately register. But when that child calls out the given name of the father, his attention is captured. That given name becomes quite helpful.

The child knows and is convinced that the person and ability portrayed by the names and their characteristics – person, provider, protector, comforter, etc. – will come through each and every time. This is not to indicate that our heavenly Father is preoccupied and may not hear us. However, awareness of His nature and ability causes us to be confident and bold when we pray, for we know the force of heaven hears and is with us.

2 Chronicles 20:15
And he said, Hearken ye, all Judah, and ye inhabitants of Jerusalem, and thou king Jehoshaphat, Thus saith the LORD unto you, Be not afraid nor dismayed by reason of this great multitude; for the battle is not yours, but God's.

Our prayers will have more impact as we incorporate the appropriate characteristic along with the boldness that comes in knowing Him in that light. **See it as being aware of the weapons in your arsenal, and then using the right weapon for the attack; that accurate force to contend *for* you.**

God is a <u>covenant</u> God. Covenant meaning agreement[1]; binding agreement[2].

The Lord Himself has made a binding agreement to us to be all He is, to us and for us. He has revealed Himself, His nature by the names He has given to describe Himself. In so doing He reveals the elements and power of the agreement. As we study the Names of God with purpose, to gain understanding, we can clearly see that we do not *allow* Him to be all He *intends* to be in our lives. Unfortunately, we sometimes limit God in what He can do in our life by assessing Him based on our encounters with natural man, our observations, and what we are taught.

God told Moses, "I AM THAT I AM". *(Exodus 3:14)*

As God's children, through the covenant, our Father promises to be:

- <u>Whatever</u> we are in need of at any given point in time

- <u>All</u> we need Him to be

- "<u>That</u>" – the necessary thing as found in His Names, His character, His capabilities.

Scriptures are oftentimes quickly claimed and confessed:

Philippians 4:13
I can do all things through Christ which strengtheneth me.

Romans 8:37
Nay, in all these things we are more than conquerors through Him that loved us.

Philippians 4:19
But my God shall supply all your need according to His riches in glory by Christ Jesus.

These are all true, but just to quote them reminds me of the scenario of the child's general call – even in all its truth, without really knowing and understanding the depth of God's capabilities, and of all we are entitled through all He is, we are pretty much making a general call hoping it all works out. (*Thank God for His grace that covers and keeps us moving along until we mature in Him.*) But when we call with confidence in the specific Name of God, grounded in the revelation of the particular characteristic that addresses an expressed need or desire, we can be assured of the God-kind of outcome.

God knows who He is and what He can do. It is up to each of us to set out to align our hearts with these truths by getting personally acquainted with Him, which galvanizes our faith. Having understanding of the specific Names and characteristics of God in our hearts; and calling on and incorporating them in our prayers is for our sake. It girds us up, builds, and sets our confidence in what He will do. Without the "revelatory" knowledge or understanding of Who He is, His Names, His character, or the covenant we have with Him we can be seduced by the enemy into believing his lies, or into not walking and operating in our full potential in God through Jesus Christ.

As New Creations, through our acceptance of Jesus Christ as Lord and Savior, we have a covenant with God, giving us access and entitlement to Him and all He is. We will look at this in greater detail in the next section – "Getting Acquainted with Jesus."

B. IT IS IN ~~THE~~ *THE* NAME

Let's take a look at some of the Names of Jehovah God. As you review the alphabetical listing of Names, notice the descriptive characteristic stated for that Name.

El-Elyon: the Most High God.
Psalm 91:1
He that dwelleth in the secret place of the Most High shall abide under the shadow of the Almighty.

There is none higher than God. He is above *all* things. There is no person, place or thing greater than the Lord, our God.

El-Shaddai: the All-Sufficient One.
Genesis 17:1
And when Abram was ninety years old and nine, the Lord appeared to Abram, and said unto him, I am the Almighty God; walk before me, and be thou perfect. And I will make My

covenant between Me and thee, and will multiply thee exceedingly.

Genesis 49:25
Even by the God of thy father, who shall help thee; and by the Almighty, who shall bless thee with blessings of heaven above, blessings of the deep that lieth under, blessings of the breasts, and of the womb...

He is more than enough. In Him you not only have your needs supplied, but you have an abundance – enough for yourself yes, but also to be a blessing to others in His Name and for His glory. See yourself as His distribution center – always full, ready to give, and always replenished.

Jesus tells us in John 10:10-11:
[10] ...I am come that they might have life, and that they might have it more abundantly.

[11] I am the Good Shepherd: the Good Shepherd giveth His life for the sheep.

Elohim: the Lord God who is the Creator.
John 1:3
All things were made by Him; and without Him was not any thing made that was made.

Genesis 1:31
And God saw every thing that He had made, and, behold, it was very good.

He is the Creator of the heavens and the earth and all that is in them.

<u>Jehovah-adonai</u>: the Lord God who is Master.
Numbers 15:41
I am the LORD your God, which brought you out of the land of Egypt, to be your God: I am the LORD your God.

Exodus 20:3
Thou shalt have no other gods before Me.

We are the servants of God. He is the One we are to obey. He is Master and there is to be no other Master in our lives aside from or along with Him. Luke 16:13 tells us that "no servant can serve two masters: for either he will hate the one, and love the other; or else he will hold to the one, and despise the other." We must all personally make a choice. I implore you to choose God and allow Him to be your Master.

<u>Jehovah-jireh</u>: the Lord God who is my Provider; He sees and provides.
Genesis 22:14
And Abraham called the name of that place Jehovah-jireh: as it is said to this day, In the mount of the Lord it shall be seen.

2 Corinthians 9:8 *Amplified Bible*
And God is able to make all grace (every favor and earthly blessing) come to you in abundance, so that you may always *and* under all circumstances *and* whatever the need be self-sufficient [possessing enough to require no aid or support and furnished in abundance for every good work and charitable donation].

In Hebrew this Name literally means "He is a God whose provision shall be seen." He provides for us in every aspect of our being – spiritually, emotionally, financially, socially and morally. He *causes* our provision. He is willing and more than able to meet our every need. It is what He does. It is who He is.

<u>Jehovah-m'kaddesh</u>: the Lord who sanctifies; sets apart.
Leviticus 20:7-8
[7] Sanctify yourselves therefore, and be ye holy: for I am the Lord your God.

[8] And ye shall keep My statutes, and do them: I am the Lord which sanctify you.

Because of the nature of the Lord – righteousness, holiness, omniscience, omnipotence, omnipresence – He is set apart from all else. There is no person, place or thing like Him. Through Salvation, we are set apart for and by Him as He has called us out of darkness and into His marvelous light. *(1 Peter 2:9)*. You are called by Him, and unto Him. You are His special treasure.

<u>Jehovah-nissi</u>: the Lord God who is our Victory Banner.
Exodus 17:15-16
[15] And Moses built an altar, and called the name of it Jehovah-nissi:

[16] For he said, Because the Lord hath sworn that the Lord will have war with Amalek from generation to generation.

Our Father is a God of victory. He only has victory in Him. 1 Timothy 6:12 tells us to fight the "good fight of faith;" well the fight, for us, is good because we are on the side of Victory Himself. When we invite the Lord into the situation, allowing Him to come in, giving Him permission, relinquishing our "control" of things to Him – then there is *definite* victory.

<u>Jehovah-rapha</u>: the Lord God who heals; Jehovah the Healer.
Exodus 15:26
And said, If thou wilt diligently hearken to the voice of the Lord thy God, and wilt do that which is right in His sight, and wilt

give ear to His commandments, and keep all His statutes, I will put none of these diseases upon thee, which I have brought upon the Egyptians: for I am the Lord that healeth thee.

Psalm 103:3
Who forgiveth all thine iniquities; who healeth all thy diseases...

In the Old Testament God said, "I am the Lord who healeth thee." In the New Testament we see many instances where Jesus went about healing them all. And for us today, by His stripes *(the wounds He sustained when He was beaten)* we are healed. It is His will for us to be healed and whole.

Jehovah-rohi: the Lord is my Shepherd; He is my Shepherd.
Psalm 23:1
The Lord is my shepherd; I shall not want.

With the Lord as our Shepherd, we do not want *(lack)*; He comforts and leads us in the paths of righteousness. He leads us in the way that is right – to go, do, say and acquire – as we relinquish our control and will to Him; setting our heart to follow His lead.

Jehovah-shalom: the Lord of peace.
Judges 6:23-24
²³ And the Lord said unto him, Peace be unto thee; fear not: thou shalt not die.

²⁴ Then Gideon built an altar there unto the Lord, and called it Jehovah-shalom: unto this day it is yet in Ophrah of the Abiezrites.

John 14:27
Peace I leave with you, my peace I give unto you: not as the world giveth, give I unto you. Let not your heart be troubled, neither let it be afraid.

This peace here is from the Hebrew word "shalom," which is defined as: well, happy, friendly, welfare, prosperity, health, favor, rest, peace, wholly[3]. We can see that it is much richer than a passing greeting with a smile pasted on our face.

God's peace is not conditional. It is not determined by the status of a situation. It is always available to you. When you keep your mind on Him, His peace will overtake you, even in the midst of the storm. *(Isaiah 26:3; Philippians 4:7)*

<u>Jehovah-shammah</u>: the Lord God who is always there; the Lord God who is present.
Ezekiel 48:35
It was round about eighteen thousand measures: and the name of the city from that day shall be, The Lord is there.

Hebrews 13:5
Let your conversation be without covetousness; and be content with such things as ye have: for He hath said, I will never leave thee, nor forsake thee.

If you know Him as Jehovah-shammah, you will know that you never have to be lonely. He is the Lord God who is always present, always there.

<u>Jehovah-tsidkenu</u>: the Lord our righteousness, God who is righteous.

Jeremiah 23:6
In his days Judah shall be saved, and Israel shall dwell safely: and this is His Name whereby He shall be called, the Lord our Righteousness.

God is virtuous, holy, and pure; having no guile or evil in Him. He is Righteousness.

C. PRAYING THE NAME(S) OF GOD

Consider this, everything God said He is in the Old Testament *(or Old Covenant)*, as described through those Names, still holds true. He is alive and real for us, in our time. All He revealed Himself to be through His Names then, He is all that for us today and forever. When we pray the Names of the Lord, we set the foundation of our heart on all *He* is, and not on the issue. Praying with the knowledge of the corresponding characteristic of the Lord causes a boldness to rise up in us from the security we have in knowing what He can, will and does do.

When the three Hebrew young men – Shadrach, Meshach and Abednego – were facing the fiery furnace and death, without hesitation they confidently declared, "Our God whom we serve is able to deliver us from the burning fiery furnace, and He <u>will</u> deliver us out of thine hand, O king." *(Daniel 3:16-17; emphasis added)* They knew the Lord as "Jehovah-adonai"– the Lord God who is Master, and "Jehovah-nissi" – the Lord God who is our Victory Banner; and as a result they experienced "Jehovah-shalom," having His peace. They were empowered to make a bold statement of sure rescue by God's mighty hand. Their confidence came by knowing God in and from the heart. We also see in this Biblical example that there is more than one Name that may suit a situation.

The same is for us, His children, today. When we call, relying on the express characteristic of God that corresponds with a specific need or desire, rooted in the revelation of THAT (*I AM THAT I AM*), we can be assured of God's outcome. We are kept mindful of the greatness of our God.

D. PRACTICAL APPLICATION

Let's put this into practice by selecting and incorporating the Name(s) of the Lord into prayers.

1. Using the list of the Names of the Lord, apply the appropriate Name for each issue listed below. There may be more than one Name that fits the situation.

- Bad doctor's report

  _____

- More bills/debt than money

  _____

- Time to take a step (or leap) of faith

  _____

2. Use this principle to fortify your prayer regarding your own personal matter. Find the appropriate Name(s) to incorporate in your prayer or declaration of truth.

EXAMPLE

Situation: Single *(unmarried)*
Name(s) of God: Jehovah-shammah, Jehovah-rohi, El-Shaddai
Prayer/Declaration:

Lord, You are Jehovah-shammah in my life; You
are ever present. I am not lonely, nor afraid and
do not dread being single because You are always
with me. Thank You for being my Companion;
my All. You are my Shepherd, Jehovah-rohi, and
El-Shaddai, supplying and leading me in all
things. Thank You. In the Name of Jesus.
Amen.

Please be assured that none of this is to complicate things for us.
God is very simplistic – He informs, we know; He instructs, we
do. Being familiar with His Names is to enhance our
understanding of Him, not to confound. Also, be certain of this,
the love of God is so powerful and all-encompassing that just to
call out, "Father," God wraps Himself around us like a warm
covering on a chilly night, and all else fades from us – all manner
of fear and loneliness dissipate – for Love, our Dad is here.

CHAPTER III

JEHOVAH AS FATHER

JEHOVAH AS FATHER

Our heart conforms to be like God as we receive more and more revelation of who He is. We grow in Him through:

- Having a relationship with Him by Jesus Christ *(Salvation)*

- Reading and meditating on the Bible *(the Word of God)*

- Prayer *(conversing with Him)*

- Utilizing the various tools offered

- Prayer, praise and worship of Him

And yes, I am going there…
- Fasting

There are many "tools" available to us to assist in our personal growth in the Lord, such as the wide assortment of Bible versions, books, study helps, seminars, conferences, workshops and classes – use them as prompted or initiated by the Holy Spirit. Tools and aids are great, but they are _never_ to replace spending personal time with your heavenly Father through His Word, in prayer, praise and worship.

In getting acquainted with Jehovah as Father we are transformed *from* hoping and wishing, *to* SURE, BOLD and CONFIDENT.

- *From*: God created the heavens and the earth
  To: GOD CREATED THE HEAVENS AND THE EARTH

That's right, put some bass in your voice; some confidence and authority in it.

- *From*: God said let there be and there was
  To: GOD SAID LET THERE BE, AND THERE WAS

- *From*: God, please help me
  To: LORD, YOU WHO ARE JEHOVAH-SHAMMAH, ARE EVER WITH ME; I SHALL NOT FEAR

Psalm 91 *King James Version*
¹ He that dwelleth in the secret place of the most High shall abide under the shadow of the Almighty.

² I will say of the LORD, He is my refuge and my fortress: my God; in Him will I trust.

³ Surely He shall deliver thee from the snare of the fowler, and from the noisome pestilence.

⁴ He shall cover thee with His feathers, and under His wings shalt thou trust: His truth shall be thy shield and buckler.

⁵ Thou shalt not be afraid for the terror by night; nor for the arrow that flieth by day;

⁶ Nor for the pestilence that walketh in darkness; nor for the destruction that wasteth at noonday.

⁷ A thousand shall fall at thy side, and ten thousand at thy right hand; but it shall not come nigh thee.

⁸ Only with thine eyes shalt thou behold and see the reward of the wicked.

⁹ Because thou hast made the LORD, which is my refuge, even the most High, thy habitation;

¹⁰ There shall no evil befall thee, neither shall any plague come nigh thy dwelling.

¹¹ For He shall give his angels charge over thee, to keep thee in all thy ways.

¹² They shall bear thee up in their hands, lest thou dash thy foot against a stone.

¹³ Thou shalt tread upon the lion and adder: the young lion and the dragon shalt thou trample under feet.

¹⁴ Because he hath set his love upon Me, therefore will I deliver him: I will set him on high, because he hath known My Name.

¹⁵ He shall call upon Me, and I will answer him: I will be with him in trouble; I will deliver him, and honour him.

¹⁶ With long life will I satisfy him, and shew him My salvation.

Now let's look at Psalm 91 in the *Amplified Bible*
¹ HE WHO dwells in the secret place of the Most High shall remain stable and fixed under the shadow of the Almighty [Whose power no foe can withstand].

² I will say of the Lord, He is my Refuge and my Fortress, my God; on Him I lean and rely, and in Him I [confidently] trust!

³ For [then] He will deliver you from the snare of the fowler and from the deadly pestilence.

⁴ [Then] He will cover you with His pinions, and under His wings shall you trust and find refuge; His truth and His faithfulness are a shield and a buckler.

⁵ You shall not be afraid of the terror of the night, nor of the arrow (the evil plots and slanders of the wicked) that flies by day,

⁶ Nor of the pestilence that stalks in darkness, nor of the destruction and sudden death that surprise and lay waste at noonday.

⁷ A thousand may fall at your side, and ten thousand at your right hand, but it shall not come near you.

⁸ Only a spectator shall you be [yourself inaccessible in the secret place of the Most High] as you witness the reward of the wicked.

⁹ Because you have made the Lord your refuge, and the Most High your dwelling place,

¹⁰ There shall no evil befall you, nor any plague or calamity come near your tent.

¹¹ For He will give His angels [especial] charge over you to accompany and defend and preserve you in all your ways [of obedience and service].

¹² They shall bear you up on their hands, lest you dash your foot against a stone.

¹³ You shall tread upon the lion and adder; the young lion and the serpent shall you trample underfoot.

¹⁴ Because he has set his love upon Me, therefore will I deliver him; I will set him on high, because he knows and understands My name [has a personal knowledge of My mercy, love, and

kindness--trusts and relies on Me, knowing I will never forsake him, no, never].

¹⁵ He shall call upon Me, and I will answer him; I will be with him in trouble, I will deliver him and honor him.

¹⁶ With long life will I satisfy him and show him My salvation.

(Here, in reading Psalm 91 in the King James Version and the Amplified Bible, we have an example of utilizing different versions of the Bible to gain even greater insight into the Lord's heart toward us.)

There is power in being in intimate fellowship with the Lord. We can see how getting acquainted with Jehovah, being intimately familiar with Him amplifies, solidifies, and gives greater depth of understanding and relationship with and in Him. There is nothing lacking or missing when we truly make Him Lord.

CHAPTER IV

THE FALL

<u>THE FALL</u>

The fall of man by Adam is how sin entered into the world, affecting the earth and all of mankind.

Genesis 3:1-19
[1] Now the serpent was more subtil than any beast of the field which the LORD God had made. And he said unto the woman, Yea, hath God said, Ye shall not eat of every tree of the garden?

[2] And the woman said unto the serpent, We may eat of the fruit of the trees of the garden:

[3] But of the fruit of the tree which is in the midst of the garden, God hath said, Ye shall not eat of it, neither shall ye touch it, lest ye die.

[4] And the serpent said unto the woman, Ye shall not surely die:

[5] For God doth know that in the day ye eat thereof, then your eyes shall be opened, and ye shall be as gods, knowing good and evil.

[6] And when the woman saw that the tree was good for food, and that it was pleasant to the eyes, and a tree to be desired to make one wise, she took of the fruit thereof, and did eat, and gave also unto her husband with her; and he did eat.

[7] And the eyes of them both were opened, and they knew that they were naked; and they sewed fig leaves together, and made themselves aprons.

⁸ And they heard the voice of the LORD God walking in the garden in the cool of the day: and Adam and his wife hid themselves from the presence of the LORD God amongst the trees of the garden.

⁹ And the LORD God called unto Adam, and said unto him, Where art thou?

¹⁰ And he said, I heard thy voice in the garden, and I was afraid, because I was naked; and I hid myself.

¹¹ And He said, Who told thee that thou wast naked? Hast thou eaten of the tree, whereof I commanded thee that thou shouldest not eat?

¹² And the man said, The woman whom thou gavest to be with me, she gave me of the tree, and I did eat.

¹³ And the LORD God said unto the woman, What is this that thou hast done? And the woman said, The serpent beguiled me, and I did eat.

¹⁴ And the LORD God said unto the serpent, Because thou hast done this, thou art cursed above all cattle, and above every beast of the field; upon thy belly shalt thou go, and dust shalt thou eat all the days of thy life:

¹⁵ And I will put enmity between thee and the woman, and between thy seed and her seed; it shall bruise thy head, and thou shalt bruise his heel.

¹⁶ Unto the woman He said, I will greatly multiply thy sorrow and thy conception; in sorrow thou shalt bring forth children; and thy desire shall be to thy husband, and he shall rule over thee.

¹⁷ And unto Adam He said, Because thou hast hearkened unto the voice of thy wife, and hast eaten of the tree, of which I

commanded thee, saying, Thou shalt not eat of it: cursed is the ground for thy sake; in sorrow shalt thou eat of it all the days of thy life;

[18] Thorns also and thistles shall it bring forth to thee; and thou shalt eat the herb of the field;

[19] In the sweat of thy face shalt thou eat bread, till thou return unto the ground; for out of it wast thou taken: for dust thou art, and unto dust shalt thou return.

Well, that is pretty self-explanatory.

Religion and tradition have given the impression, have taught and even allowed for the joking that Eve acted alone in the Garden of Eden, to hinder the understanding of the power of the redemption explanation of the following verses.

Romans 5:12
[20] Wherefore, as by one man sin entered into the world, and death by sin; and so death passed upon all men, for that all have sinned.

1 Corinthians 15:21-22
[21] For since by man came death, by man came also the resurrection of the dead.

[22] For as in Adam all die, even so in Christ shall all be made alive.

However, Genesis 3:6 tells us that Adam was with her. You see, the devil uses deception and distraction to keep us from realizing the potency of God's redemptive work, attempting to keep us in the dark this way:

If we think and focus on Eve as a lone culprit, the reality of Adam's role in the fall is diminished significantly. The devil further deceives with insinuations to our subconscious, setting off "reasonings" that if Adam's part in the fall is insignificant and possibly inaccurate, then the entire recounting through these verses, including Christ's role in the redemption, is insignificant and possibly inaccurate as well.

As no one would ever consciously think or speak that aloud, satan's deception goes unchecked, even causing us to skip over the divine significance and finality of the redemption of mankind; and thus diluting the truth. However, no attempt, plan or scheme of satan is greater than the truth of God's Word – by one man *(Adam)* all die; by one Man *(JESUS)* all are made alive. Amen.

CHAPTER V

BY HIS GREAT LOVE –
A REDEEMER IS PROMISED
AND DELIVERED

By His Great Love – A Redeemer Is Promised and Delivered

By God's great love, He promises *and* delivers a Redeemer. It is His mercy that established and implemented the plan of restoration. Mercy is of the heart and power of God to forgive and remove the effects of sin. Redemption is of His kindness, compassion, favor, love and forbearance.

At the issuance of the curse brought on by the "fall of man" we see a testimony of Adam's confidence in God, established by their closeness. We are provided a glimpse into Adam's heart regarding His knowledge of God. Adam expresses hope and faith in the faithfulness of God, even in his fallen state, in naming his wife Eve.

Genesis 3:20
And Adam called his wife's name Eve; because she was
the mother of all living.

And God responds with acts of love, and in faithfulness to what He had set in order before the foundation of the world: for man, created in His own likeness, to operate as He in dominion and authority as stewards of the earth.

Genesis 3:21-24 *Amplified Bible*
²¹ For Adam also and for his wife the Lord God made long coats (tunics) of skins and clothed them.

²² And the Lord God said, Behold, the man has become like one of Us [the Father, Son, and Holy Spirit], to know [how to distinguish between] good and evil and blessing and calamity; and now, lest he put forth his hand and take also from the tree of life and eat, and live forever –

²³ Therefore the Lord God sent him forth from the Garden of Eden to till the ground from which he was taken.

²⁴ So [God] drove out the man; and He placed at the east of the Garden of Eden the cherubim and a flaming sword which turned every way, to keep and guard the way to the tree of life.

In His faithfulness to all He is, the Lord set things in order:

- He provided the first sin offering – in providing the skins to cover Adam and Eve's nakedness, the animal's blood was shed, which atoned for *(covering but not eliminating)* the sin.

- He evicted Adam and Eve from the Garden – curse, yes; but we also see that the Lord proceeded in mercy, providing protection in evicting them so they would not eat of the Tree of Life, which would have caused them to live forever.

But, you may be thinking, through Salvation we are to live forever. Right? Right! Conflict here? No way.

The point and purpose regarding Adam and Eve's eviction and guarding against their eating of the Tree of Life, was for them not to live forever in that cursed state and sin condition, and thereby setting no way of escape or restoration. Had they stayed and eaten from the Tree of Life they would have been locked and sealed in that condition, making it unalterable, and inevitably passing that final state on to us and those after. Therefore, the Lord secured things until the One, True and Appropriate offering could be made – that offering being Jesus Christ, which only by Him and His shed blood is sin removed. Hallelujah!

Because of Adam's act of sin, all of mankind was cursed.

This is confirmed by Romans 5:12 *New International Version.*

> Therefore, just as sin entered into the world through one man, and death through sin, in this way death came to all men…

But all was not lost; for there was a promise and its fulfillment made to mankind by God, of a Savior, a Redeemer – Jesus Christ.

Genesis 3:15
And I will put enmity between thee and the woman, and between thy seed and her seed; it shall bruise thy head, and thou shalt bruise his heel.

Isaiah 9:6-7
[6] For unto us a Child is born, unto us a Son is given: and the government shall be upon His shoulder: and His name shall be called Wonderful, Counseller, The mighty God, The everlasting Father, The Prince of Peace.

[7] Of the increase of His government and peace there shall be no end, upon the throne of David, and upon his kingdom, to order it, and to stablish it with judgment and with justice from henceforth even for ever. The zeal of the LORD of hosts will perform this.

Romans 16:20
And the God of peace shall bruise Satan under your feet shortly.
The grace of our Lord Jesus Christ be with you. Amen.

1 Corinthians 15:21-22 *New International Version* explains:
[21] For since death came through a man, the resurrection of the
dead comes also through a Man.

[22] For as in Adam all die, so in Christ all will be made alive.

And so it was, Jesus the Redeemer was born; and the restoration
of mankind to the Father was initiated. Glory to God!

As there was the "fall of mankind" by Adam; the mumbling,
grumbling, complaining and sinning against God in the
wilderness by the Israelites; and even though we ourselves have
our own personal issues of sin and disobedience, the Lord God
our Father, remains faithful to who He is, His covenant, and to
us, His children, extending mercy from on high. Hallelujah!

God's biggest and greatest promise is that of SALVATION,
which includes our redemption – the payment of the price
incurred by sin, by Adam, as well as our own.

Romans 6:23
For the wages of sin is death; but the gift of God is eternal life
through Jesus Christ our Lord.

Salvation is our accepting Jesus Christ as Savior; and full
appropriation of ALL its privileges and benefits is contingent on
our making Him the Lord of our life. *(In the next Section we will
endeavor to become more acquainted with Jesus Christ.)*

REFLECTIONS

The Lord's desire is that we see and consider Him, not only as GOD but as LORD; not only as LORD but also as FATHER, and then on to DAD. Father is intimate; and Dad even more so. **We are to have an up-close-and-personal relationship with the Lord.** This involves fellowshipping with Him through prayer, reading and meditating on His Word, fasting, worshiping and praising Him, which, as we are told in many of the Psalms, is the way into His presence, into His gates, and into His courts.

Ponder this:

God pursuing you...wooing you. In His Word, He tells you how much He loves you, and what He will do; not only for you but also your generations. He tells you that He is a real, live Being. He assures that He will not lie to you or let you down. He introduces Himself to you through His Word. Glory to God!

In really knowing God we are more apt to respect, obey and believe Him; His Word becomes ours; and His promises to us take root in our heart. This is how we are able to continue standing, confessing and declaring what He says about matters. We can better and more sincerely witness to others *(tell them about Him)*, as it is easier to introduce and share about someone with whom you are well acquainted.

Let me encourage you to be specific in your prayer life. Consider and use God's Names when you pray. They reveal who He is, His character and what He can and will do, while keeping you stirred up and bold in Him. Remember, you are praying to a living God. He hears, answers and does.

Relinquish, surrender your will, plans and goals to Him; submit to His ways, realizing and admitting that you can do nothing without Him...not even breathe.

Selah *(pause and seriously consider that)*

SECTION TWO

GETTING ACQUAINTED WITH JESUS

<u>FOUNDATION SCRIPTURES:</u>
1 Timothy 3:16
And without controversy great is the mystery of godliness: God was manifest in the flesh, justified in the Spirit, seen of angels, preached unto the Gentiles, believed on in the world, received up in glory.

John 10:10
I and My Father are One.

1 John 5:11
And this is the record, that God hath given to us eternal life, and this life is in His Son.

<u>INTRODUCTION</u>
In this section we will consider the depth of God's love through the promised Redeemer. Jesus, the fulfillment of that promise,

is our Redeemer, Savior, Christ, Counselor, Prince of Peace, King of kings and Lord of lords.

In intimately getting acquainted with Jesus:

- Your confidence and assurance are substantially built.

- You come to know that the Father's love for you is absolute, as you realize how great the sacrifice was.

- You gain the understanding that the goodness, faithfulness and great love the Father has for you are conveyed through Jesus, His Son, and by His Blood.

- You come to know that the promises and teachings of the Father, expressed in His Word, are not light sayings only for consideration; but they are real, for you, and to be utilized in your life.

- You come to know Jesus as the Christ *(the Anointed One)*; and that He is real and alive.

To know "<u>intimately</u>" is to know thoroughly; through and through; very well; fully; in detail. It is defined as "most personal; very familiar[1]." This intimacy is where your victory...your peace...your joy...your success...your blessing lie.

When you KNOW who Jesus is, in conjunction with KNOWING who the Father is, you can KNOW who you are – as a New Creature in Christ – and the impact of being in Him.

- You can stop "hoping" things work out and begin standing, operating and living fully assured that it is already work<u>ed</u> out.

- You can wait on the Lord in patience and peace for manifestation of His answers and promises with certainty.

- You can confidently follow His direction.

When you KNOW that the Father and Jesus are One and that that "One" lives in you by the Holy Spirit you can see yourself as:

- "More than conquerors" (*Romans 8:37*)

- "The head and not the tail; above and not beneath" (*Deuteronomy 28:13*)

- "Blessed in the city; blessed in the field" (*Deuteronomy 28:3*)

- "Blessed coming in; blessed going out" (*Deuteronomy 28:6*)

- You are unashamedly <u>sure</u> that everything you set your hands to shall prosper. (*Deuteronomy 28:8*)

Declare aloud: "**God lives in me!**"
Hallelujah!

CHAPTER I

JESUS, SON OF GOD

JESUS, SON OF GOD

John 1:1-18
¹ In the beginning was the Word, and the Word was with God, and the Word was God.

² The same was in the beginning with God.

³ All things were made by Him; and without Him was not any thing made that was made.

⁴ In Him was Life; and the Life was the Light of men.

⁵ And the Light shineth in darkness; and the darkness comprehended it not.

⁶ There was a man sent from God, whose name was John.

⁷ The same came for a witness, to bear witness of the Light, that all men through Him might believe.

⁸ He was not that Light, but was sent to bear witness of that Light.

⁹ That was the true Light, which lighteth every man that cometh into the world.

¹⁰ He was in the world, and the world was made by Him, and the world knew Him not.

¹¹ He came unto His own, and His own received Him not.

[12] But as many as received Him, to them gave He power to become the sons of God, even to them that believe on His Name:

[13] Which were born, not of blood, nor of the will of the flesh, nor of the will of man, but of God.

[14] And the Word was made flesh, and dwelt among us, (and we beheld His glory, the glory as of the only begotten of the Father,) full of grace and truth.

[15] John bare witness of Him, and cried, saying, This was He of whom I spake, He that cometh after me is preferred before me: for He was before me.

[16] And of His fullness have all we received, and grace for grace.

[17] For the law was given by Moses, but grace and truth came by Jesus Christ.

[18] No man hath seen God at any time; the only begotten Son, which is in the bosom of the Father, He hath declared Him.

One of the most important titles Jesus held is that of "Logos," which means "Word". God reveals Himself to us by His Word. He expressed His love to us by, in and through Jesus Christ, His Son, whom He sent to earth for the redemption of all mankind. While on earth, Jesus was fully God and fully man – being God manifested in the flesh.

John 10:30
I and My Father are One.

John 5:18
Therefore the Jews sought the more to kill Him, because He not only had broken the Sabbath, but said also that God was His Father, making Himself equal with God.

At no time did Jesus cease being God. As part of the Godhead, He is due the same honor as God, the Father. In fulfilling the will of the Father, He was made flesh; suffered every temptation as a man, yet never sinned Himself; and experienced spiritual death so we would not have to. This spiritual death was separation from the Father, initiated by Adam at the fall of man, which Jesus suffered for us, in our place. Through His *(Jesus')* own physical death, burial, resurrection and ascension, satan, and his darkness were defeated. It is through Jesus that *we* have victory over satan, his agents and schemes.

When we look at all this as a complete package, we see that **God...the Word...His Love...and Christ are all One**, presented to us to accept and be forever redeemed and forever changed.

Matthew 26:53-54
[53] Thinkest thou that I cannot now pray to My Father, and He shall presently give Me more than twelve legions of angels?

[54] But how then shall the Scriptures be fulfilled, that thus it must be?

John 14:6
Jesus saith unto him, I am the Way, the Truth, and the Life: no man cometh unto the Father, but by Me.

John 10:10b
...I am come that they might have life, and that they might have it more abundantly.

Through and by Jesus we have life, eternal life which begins at Salvation. He could give life because He is Life; life is His to give.

John 3:16-17

16 For God so loved the world, that He gave His only begotten Son, that whosoever believeth in Him should not perish, but have everlasting life.

17 For God sent not His Son into the world to condemn the world; but that the world through Him might be saved.

God's giving of Himself by way of and in the person of Jesus, giving His own life was based on love...love for the world...love for you, (insert your name here).

The following Names refer to different aspects of Jesus:
- "Son of God," His Divine name

- "Son of David," His Jewish name

- "Son of Man" acknowledges the humanity of Christ; using it to identify Himself with humanity

John 5:19-27

19 Then answered Jesus and said unto them, Verily, verily, I say unto you, The Son can do nothing of Himself, but what He seeth the Father do: for what things soever He doeth, these also doeth the Son likewise.

20 For the Father loveth the Son, and sheweth Him all things that Himself doeth: and He will shew Him greater works than these, that ye may marvel.

²¹ For as the Father raiseth up the dead, and quickeneth them; even so the Son quickeneth whom He will.

²² For the Father judgeth no man, but hath committed all judgment unto the Son:

²³ That all men should honour the Son, even as they honour the Father. He that honoureth not the Son honoureth not the Father which hath sent Him.

²⁴ Verily, verily, I say unto you, He that heareth my word, and believeth on Him that sent me, hath everlasting life, and shall not come into condemnation; but is passed from death unto life.

²⁵ Verily, verily, I say unto you, The hour is coming, and now is, when the dead shall hear the voice of the Son of God: and they that hear shall live.

²⁶ For as the Father hath life in Himself; so hath He given to the Son to have life in Himself;

²⁷ And hath given Him authority to execute judgment also, because He is the Son of Man.

By identifying Himself as "Son of Man," as in <u>mankind</u>, God makes the point that Jesus' Lordship, Sonship and Divinity were not limited to the Jews, but was for <u>all</u>. It qualifies Him as the substitution for mankind in God's plan of redemption. He came to earth, gave His life and rose from the dead for all mankind; however, it is up to every individual to make the decision to accept Him, the great sacrifice He made, and become His very own.

As "Son of Man," Jesus was qualified to shed His blood for the sin of mankind and stand in judgment in our place, in substitution for us. The humanity of Jesus also establishes that

He was qualified to be a compassionate and faithful High Priest, to go before the Father on our behalf, in His compassion for us.

John 5:43a
I am come in My Father's Name...

John 20:31
But these are written, that ye might believe that Jesus is the Christ, the Son of God; and that believing ye might have life through His Name.

God, in His magnificent plan of redemption – to reconcile mankind back to Himself through payment of the penalty incurred by sin; restoring us back to man's original condition *prior* to the fall – gave of Himself through His Son, Jesus, the Christ. No other sacrifice, no other blood was powerful enough to satisfy such a huge debt.

Let's consider the term "redemption" to better grasp our standing as New Creatures. Redemption is explained as deliverance, rescue; atonement for guilt; repurchase, as of something sold, paying off as of a note or bond; recovery by payment, as of something pledged; releasing, ransoming; to buy back.

That debt incurred against man as a result of sin is paid in full by the shed Blood of Jesus Christ; delivering us *from* the grip of darkness and ownership of the devil, and *into* the marvelous light and possession of the Lord God.

The magnitude of God's plan – once and for all mankind: those then, now *and* yet to come – required more than the blood of animals. Only the Blood of Jesus, the Son of God; the Blood of God Himself, could suffice: powerful enough to wash away sin, which, prior to the sacrifice of Jesus, could only be covered in using the blood of animals for atonement.

CHAPTER II

JESUS, HIGH PRIEST

JESUS, HIGH PRIEST

Hebrews 4:14-16, 5:1-10 *Amplified Bible*

¹⁴ Inasmuch then as we have a great High Priest Who has [already] ascended and passed through the heavens, Jesus the Son of God, let us hold fast our confession [of faith in Him].

¹⁵ For we do not have a High Priest Who is unable to understand and sympathize and have a shared feeling with our weaknesses and infirmities and liability to the assaults of temptation, but One Who has been tempted in every respect as we are, yet without sinning.

¹⁶ Let us then fearlessly and confidently and boldly draw near to the throne of grace (the throne of God's unmerited favor to us sinners), that we may receive mercy [for our failures] and find grace to help in good time for every need [appropriate help and well-timed help, coming just when we need it].

⁵:¹ FOR EVERY high priest chosen from among men is appointed to act on behalf of men in things relating to God, to offer both gifts and sacrifices for sins.

² He is able to exercise gentleness and forbearance toward the ignorant and erring, since he himself also is liable to moral weakness and physical infirmity.

³ And because of this he is obliged to offer sacrifice for his own sins, as well as for those of the people.

⁴ Besides, one does not appropriate for himself the honor [of being high priest], but he is called by God and receives it of Him, just as Aaron did.

⁵ So too Christ (the Messiah) did not exalt Himself to be made a high priest, but was appointed and exalted by Him Who said to Him, You are My Son; today I have begotten You;

⁶ As He says also in another place, You are a Priest [appointed] forever after the order (with the rank) of Melchizedek.

⁷ In the days of His flesh [Jesus] offered up definite, special petitions [for that which He not only wanted but needed] and supplications with strong crying and tears to Him Who was [always] able to save Him [out] from death, and He was heard because of His reverence toward God [His godly fear, His piety, in that He shrank from the horrors of separation from the bright presence of the Father].

⁸ Although He was a Son, He learned [active, special] obedience through what He suffered

⁹ And, [His completed experience] making Him perfectly [equipped], He became the Author and Source of eternal salvation to all those who give heed and obey Him,

¹⁰ Being designated and recognized and saluted by God as High Priest after the order (with the rank) of Melchizedek.

(Emphasis added – v. 7)

There are three qualifications for the high priest, who, in the Old Testament, was of the family or tribe of Levi:

1. He must be chosen – called, appointed by God; he cannot promote himself to the position or office.

2. <u>He must be compassionate</u> – gentle and forbearing toward "the ignorant and erring" *(those who inadvertently sin)* – mindful that he has weaknesses also.

3. <u>He must minister on behalf of others</u> – those things pertaining to God, giving offerings and gifts to God on their behalf.

Hebrews 7:27 *Amplified Bible*
He has no day by day necessity, as [do each of these other] high priests, to offer sacrifice first of all for his own [personal] sins and then for those of the people, because He [met all the requirements] once for all when He brought Himself [as a sacrifice] which He offered up.

Jesus, the Son of God...Christ the Messiah fulfills *all* these requirements.

1. **He was chosen – <u>Jesus was divinely appointed</u>.**

Hebrews 7:11, 15-28 *Amplified Bible*
[11] Now if perfection (a perfect fellowship between God and the worshiper) had been attainable by the Levitical priesthood--for under it the people were given the Law--why was it further necessary that there should arise another and different kind of Priest, one after the order of Melchizedek, rather than one appointed after the order and rank of Aaron?

[15] And this becomes more plainly evident when another Priest arises Who bears the likeness of Melchizedek,

[16] Who has been constituted a Priest, not on the basis of a bodily legal requirement [an externally imposed command concerning His physical ancestry], but on the basis of the power of an endless and indestructible Life.

¹⁷ For it is witnessed of Him, You are a Priest forever after the order (with the rank) of Melchizedek.

¹⁸ So a previous physical regulation and command is cancelled because of its weakness and ineffectiveness and uselessness--

¹⁹ For the Law never made anything perfect--but instead a better hope is introduced through which we [now] come close to God.

²⁰ And it was not without the taking of an oath [that Christ was made Priest],

²¹ For those who formerly became priests received their office without its being confirmed by the taking of an oath by God, but this One was designated and addressed and saluted with an oath, The Lord has sworn and will not regret it or change His mind, You are a Priest forever according to the order of Melchizedek.

²² In keeping with [the oath's greater strength and force], Jesus has become the Guarantee of a better (stronger) agreement [a more excellent and more advantageous covenant].

²³ [Again, the former successive line of priests] was made up of many, because they were each prevented by death from continuing [perpetually in office];

²⁴ But He holds His priesthood unchangeably, because He lives on forever.

²⁵ Therefore He is able also to save to the uttermost (completely, perfectly, finally, and for all time and eternity) those who come to God through Him, since He is always living to make petition to God and intercede with Him and intervene for them.

²⁶ [Here is] the High Priest [perfectly adapted] to our needs, as was fitting--holy, blameless, unstained by sin, separated from sinners, and exalted higher than the heavens.

[27] He has no day by day necessity, as [do each of these other] high priests, to offer sacrifice first of all for his own [personal] sins and then for those of the people, because He [met all the requirements] once for all when He brought Himself [as a sacrifice] which He offered up.

[28] For the Law sets up men in their weakness [frail, sinful, dying human beings] as high priests, but the word of [God's] oath, which [was spoken later] after the institution of the Law, [chooses and appoints as priest One Whose appointment is complete and permanent], a Son Who has been made perfect forever.

(Emphasis added – vv. 21, 25)

2. **He was compassionate** – Jesus had compassion for others.

Hebrews 2:9-18 *Amplified Bible*
[9] But we are able to see Jesus, Who was ranked lower than the angels for a little while, crowned with glory and honor because of His having suffered death, in order that by the grace (unmerited favor) of God [to us sinners] He might experience death for every individual person.

[10] For it was an act worthy [of God] and fitting [to the divine nature] that He, for Whose sake and by Whom all things have their existence, in bringing many sons into glory, should make the Pioneer of their salvation perfect [should bring to maturity the human experience necessary to be perfectly equipped for His office as High Priest] through suffering.

[11] For both He Who sanctifies [making men holy] and those who are sanctified all have one [Father]. For this reason He is not ashamed to call them brethren;

¹² For He says, I will declare Your [the Father's] name to My brethren; in the midst of the [worshiping] congregation I will sing hymns of praise to You.

¹³ And again He says, My trust and assured reliance and confident hope shall be fixed in Him. And yet again, Here I am, I and the children whom God has given Me.

¹⁴ Since, therefore, [these His] children share in flesh and blood [in the physical nature of human beings], He [Himself] in a similar manner partook of the same [nature], that by [going through] death He might bring to naught and make of no effect him who had the power of death--that is, the devil--

¹⁵ And also that He might deliver and completely set free all those who through the [haunting] fear of death were held in bondage throughout the whole course of their lives.

¹⁶ For, as we all know, He [Christ] did not take hold of angels [the fallen angels, to give them a helping and delivering hand], but He did take hold of [the fallen] descendants of Abraham [to reach out to them a helping and delivering hand].

¹⁷ So it is evident that it was essential that He be made like His brethren in every respect, in order that He might become a merciful (sympathetic) and faithful High Priest in the things related to God, to make atonement and propitiation for the people's sins.

¹⁸ For because He Himself [in His humanity] has suffered in being tempted (tested and tried), He is able [immediately] to run to the cry of (assist, relieve) those who are being tempted and tested and tried [and who therefore are being exposed to suffering].

(Emphasis added – vv. 17-18)

Jesus, operating as human, laying aside reliance on His divinity for the allotted season to fulfill God's purpose on our behalf, became well able to relate and have compassion on humanity in His role of High Priest between God and us. As *the* compassionate High Priest, Jesus was gentle and forbearing of others, not because of any personal weaknesses or infirmities of His own – for He had none. He knew the extent of the penalty and that we could not possibly satisfy or pay it ourselves. He, having been tested and tried as a man, is able to immediately empathize, and assist and relieve us when we are tested, tried and exposed to suffering.

I am sure we can all look back and see where He, because of His great compassion for us, came to our aid even when we could not or did not call on Him. I also KNOW there are many, many instances where He steps in, with us unaware, intercepting attacks of the devil and cutting off results from acts of our own foolishness...that is MERCY.

Ponder this:

Through Salvation, *(my accepting Jesus Christ as personal Lord and Savior, God becoming my heavenly Father)*; and in spending time with Him, *(becoming intimate with Him, learning who He is and of His great love for me)*; I am aware of how precious I am to Him. As a result, I KNOW He is looking out for me, assuring His best for my life. As He is no respecter of persons, as He does for me, I know He also does for you. *(Acts 10:34)* Even when our free will comes into play, and on the occasion that we miss it, He *still* loves us back on point: to that place of repentance, where He promises to forgive when we confess our sins to Him. *(1 John 1:9)*

Thank You, Father God. Thank You.

The intensity of His compassion for us is expressed in Luke 22:39, 41-44 *Amplified Bible*:

³⁹ And He came out and went, as was His habit, to the Mount of Olives, and the disciples also followed Him.

⁴¹ And He withdrew from them about a stone's throw and knelt down and prayed,

⁴² Saying, Father, if You are willing, remove this cup from Me; yet not My will, but [always] Yours be done.

⁴³ And there appeared to Him an angel from heaven, strengthening Him in spirit.

⁴⁴ And being in an agony [of mind], He prayed [all the] more earnestly and intently, and His sweat became like great clots of blood dropping down upon the ground.

I read an explanation in one commentary that Jesus was in agony because He had to take on the sins of mankind; that He struggled with His own destiny to be made sin-bearer for all, and for all the ages.

That just did not sit right with me, and I did not see Scripture supporting that theory. I believed in my heart that as horrible as Jesus knew His mission to be, the agony came from knowing this sacrifice would require His being separated from the Father. And God confirmed it for me in two ways – a conversation with my sister; and then I "came across," *(more accurately the Holy Spirit led me to)* Hebrews 5:7 in the Amplified Bible in my reading, where the last portion of the verse states: "in that He shrank from the horrors of <u>separation from the bright presence of the Father</u>."

(This is a wonderful example, by the way, of God satisfying His child's hunger/thirst for Him, in providing the answer, confirmation and clarification through His Word. He will not have us ignorant. – Romans 11:25. Glory to God!)

I believe the intensity of Christ's intercession, substantiated and grounded in incredible love, may have sounded more like this:

> "Father, as atrocious as this assignment is, bearing the humiliation and punishment for what I did not do; having to be separated/disconnected from You – Oh, God...if there be any other way..."

> "Yet," He continued, "'The covenant established with them by Us in Genesis 3:15 and Isaiah 9:6-7 must be fulfilled. Therefore, 'not My will, but Yours be done.'"

> Then He concluded, "(_ insert your name here _) will be born and will not be able to personally pay the price required for the remission of sin, I remain committed...'not My will, but Yours be done,' Father."

Luke 23:34-43

[34] Then said Jesus, Father, forgive them; for they know not what they do. And they parted His raiment, and cast lots.

[35] And the people stood beholding. And the rulers also with them derided Him, saying, He saved others; let Him save himself, if He be Christ, the Chosen of God.

[36] And the soldiers also mocked Him, coming to Him, and offering Him vinegar,

[37] And saying, If thou be the King of the Jews, save Thyself.

[38] And a superscription also was written over Him in letters of Greek, and Latin, and Hebrew, THIS IS THE KING OF THE JEWS.

³⁹ And one of the malefactors which were hanged railed on Him, saying, If thou be Christ, save Thyself and us.

⁴⁰ But the other answering rebuked him, saying, Dost not thou fear God, seeing thou art in the same condemnation?

⁴¹ And we indeed justly; for we receive the due reward of our deeds: but this Man hath done nothing amiss.

⁴² And he said unto Jesus, Lord, remember me when thou comest into thy kingdom.

⁴³ And Jesus said unto him, Verily I say unto thee, Today shalt thou be with Me in paradise.

3. **He ministered on behalf of others** – <u>Jesus offered the best, the ultimate sacrifice: Himself.</u>

John 19:28, 30
²⁸ After this, Jesus knowing that all things were now accomplished, that the scripture might be fulfilled, saith, I thirst.

³⁰ When Jesus therefore had received the vinegar, He said, <u>It is finished</u>: and He bowed His head, and gave up the ghost.

The same love that moved Jesus to pray with such intensity in the Garden of Gethsemane (*Mark 14:32; Luke 22:44*), caused Him to remain on the cross until the assignment was complete and He said, "<u>It is finished.</u>" While there, even at the taunting of the spectators and one of the other two men being crucified, this great love caused Jesus to remain steadfast. In fact, in the midst of being crucified, He prayed *(interceded)*, asking the Father to forgive them, "For they know not what they do." (*Luke 23:34*)

Hebrews 12:2
Looking unto Jesus the Author and Finisher of our faith; who <u>for</u> <u>the joy that was set before Him endured the cross</u>, despising the shame, and is set down at the right hand of the throne of God. <i>(Emphasis added)</i>

Jesus endured the cross, remaining there for the "joy" that was set before Him. What joy? The joy in seeing…in knowing the finished product. He looked ahead to the end-result: He saw each of us…yes He saw <i>you</i>…reconciled to the Father and free from the grip of the devil; securing Salvation for you. He saw <i>your</i> face; and in seeing it before Him; His determination was this:

> "Because I know and see that the opportunity to fellowship with Us must be made available to (_insert your name here_), I will not remove Myself from this."

Now that's love. Love for you kept Him there; that was His joy. Hallelujah! Glory to God!

In the Old Testament there was an annual "Day of Atonement" – <i>this is not to be confused with the other types of offerings, some daily.</i> The Day of Atonement was when the high priest would go into the Holy of Holies, past the veil that separated the Lord from man <i>(necessitated by the fall of man)</i> and make a sin offering for himself and for the people.

In that day only the high priest could go into the Holy of Holies, where God resided <i>(as located here on earth at that time)</i>, and only on the occasion God specified. He could not go in unto the Lord whenever or however he wanted. Great preparation was required of the high priest, which even included detailed instructions for bathing and dressing. God tells Moses to tell his brother, Aaron – the high priest, that if he did not obey God's directive he would surely die just as two of his sons, the priests, Nadab and Abihu, who were killed in a flash of fire from heaven for not reverencing the Lord and His commandment. (*Leviticus 10:1-2*)

God is so holy and pure that sin cannot be associated with Him, or be in His presence. Coming into the Holy of Holies, into the presence of the Lord was intense business.

Leviticus 16:1-4
[1] And the LORD spake unto Moses after the death of the two sons of Aaron, when they offered before the LORD, and died;

[2] And the LORD said unto Moses, Speak unto Aaron thy brother, that he come not at all times into the holy place within the veil before the mercy seat, which is upon the ark; that he die not: for I will appear in the cloud upon the mercy seat.

[3] Thus shall Aaron come into the holy place: with a young bullock for a sin offering, and a ram for a burnt offering.

[4] He shall put on the holy linen coat, and he shall have the linen breeches upon his flesh, and shall be girded with a linen girdle, and with the linen mitre shall he be attired: these are holy garments; therefore shall he wash his flesh in water, and so put them on.

Verse 4 gives significance to the encounter when Jesus appeared to Mary Magdalene, telling her, "Touch me not, for I am not yet ascended to My Father..." (*John 20:17*) He was in His role or position as High Priest; washed, dressed and ready to go in unto the Lord on our behalf.

Imagine a surgeon, all scrub-brush cleaned, dressed in his "scrubs" – designated operating room attire, even down to the covering of the shoes – and ready to go in to operate. If anything touches him/her, he/she is considered contaminated and the sterilization process must be repeated.

By Jesus we have direct access to God. We can enter into His presence at and in all times – times of reward and times of challenge. We do not have to have a middleman to go in for us, or make amends for us. We can go in unto God and fellowship directly. However, we are still to reverence Him; He is always God. As we saw in the previous section, we are to regard Him as holy, esteem Him highly and respectfully..."hallowed be His Name."

CHAPTER III

JESUS, SACRIFICIAL LAMB

JESUS, SACRIFICIAL LAMB

Matthew 27:51 tells us that the veil – placed between God and us at the fall of man, enabling Him to interact with mankind in the sin state – was torn when Jesus was crucified; eliminating our separation from God. The veil was a foreshadow of Jesus' Blood. However, as the veil could only mask sin, the Blood of Jesus completely and permanently cleansed it away. We who accept Him are rendered sin-free with all separation removed. It is by His great blood sacrifice – a sin offering for us – that we are restored to a perfected position with God: of not only becoming His sons and daughters; but also with restored authority to operate as He operates, taking dominion; and being fruitful, multiplying and subduing the earth. This is the same position Adam had with God prior to his sin against Him.

Philippians 2:7-8
⁷ But made Himself (Christ Jesus) of no reputation, and took upon Him the form of a servant, and was made in the likeness of men:

⁸ And being found in fashion as a man, He humbled Himself, and became obedient unto death, even the death of the cross.

Jesus was not only the High Priest, the One to offer the sacrifice, but He was also *THE* SACRIFICE.

Leviticus 16:14-19

[14] And he shall take of the blood of the bullock, and sprinkle it with his finger upon the mercy seat eastward; and before the mercy seat shall he sprinkle of the blood with his finger seven times.

[15] Then shall he kill the goat of the sin offering, that is for the people, and bring his blood within the veil, and do with that blood as he did with the blood of the bullock, and sprinkle it upon the mercy seat, and before the mercy seat:

[16] And he shall make an atonement for the holy place, because of the uncleanness of the children of Israel, and because of their transgressions in all their sins: and so shall he do for the tabernacle of the congregation, that remaineth among them in the midst of their uncleanness.

[17] And there shall be no man in the tabernacle of the congregation when he goeth in to make an atonement in the holy place, until he come out, and have made an atonement for himself, and for his household, and for all the congregation of Israel.

[18] And he shall go out unto the altar that is before the LORD, and make an atonement for it; and shall take of the blood of the bullock, and of the blood of the goat, and put it upon the horns of the altar round about.

[19] And he shall sprinkle of the blood upon it with his finger seven times, and cleanse it, and hallow it from the uncleanness of the children of Israel.

In the process of atoning for the sins of the people, the high priest would first take the blood of a bull and spread it on the mercy seat for his own sins; and then the blood of a goat, spreading it on the mercy seat before the Lord for the sins of the people. This had to be done annually, for the blood of animals cannot remove sin; this blood could only cover up the sin from before the Lord. Think of it as being made presentable.

Testimony:
I remember an apartment my family rented – freshly prepared and painted for our moving in. They had little notes throughout to let us know they had cleaned, sanitized, removed and installed – all in preparation for the arrival of the Marshall family.

It was not until we started to unpack and put things away that we saw they had painted over cob webs and other debris. They spray painted over it all. Maintenance had readied the apartment for us, making it presentable, but only by covering up the fragments of the previous tenants and time – they only covered the past.

This is what the blood of animals did for sins; they were only covered. Our apartment, as also the children of Israel were presentable but the remains, just like their sins were still there.

Hebrews 9:6-14 *Amplified Bible*
[6] These arrangements having thus been made, the priests enter [habitually] into the outer division of the tabernacle in performance of their ritual acts of worship.

[7] But into the second [division of the tabernacle] none but the high priest goes, and he only once a year, and never without taking a sacrifice of blood with him, which he offers for himself and for the errors and sins of ignorance and thoughtlessness which the people have committed.

[8] By this the Holy Spirit points out that the way into the [true Holy of] Holies is not yet thrown open as long as the former [the outer portion of the] tabernacle remains a recognized institution and is still standing,

[9] Seeing that that first [outer portion of the] tabernacle was a parable (a visible symbol or type or picture of the present age).

In it gifts and sacrifices are offered, and yet are incapable of perfecting the conscience or of cleansing and renewing the inner man of the worshiper.

¹⁰ For [the ceremonies] deal only with clean and unclean meats and drinks and different washings, [mere] external rules and regulations for the body imposed to tide the worshipers over until the time of setting things straight [of reformation, of the complete new order when Christ, the Messiah, shall establish the reality of what these things foreshadow--a better covenant].

¹¹ But [that appointed time came] when Christ (the Messiah) appeared as a High Priest of the better things that have come and are to come. [Then] through the greater and more perfect tabernacle not made with [human] hands, that is, not a part of this material creation,

¹² He went once for all into the [Holy of] Holies [of heaven], not by virtue of the blood of goats and calves [by which to make reconciliation between God and man], but His own blood, having found and secured a complete redemption (an everlasting release for us).

¹³ For if [the mere] sprinkling of unholy and defiled persons with blood of goats and bulls and with the ashes of a burnt heifer is sufficient for the purification of the body,

¹⁴ How much more surely shall the blood of Christ, Who by virtue of [His] eternal Spirit [His own preexistent divine personality] has offered Himself as an unblemished sacrifice to God, purify our consciences from dead works and lifeless observances to serve the [ever] living God?

CHAPTER IV

ALL CHRIST IS, HE IS FOR YOU

ALL CHRIST IS, HE IS FOR YOU

All Jesus has done, with all He is, is for you. The great sacrifice of love was His giving His life so you would have eternal life with God, which begins at the moment of Salvation. He endured the humiliation for you. He remained on the cross for you. He was buried for you. He conquered satan and death for you. He rose on the third day for you. He ascended to heaven and is seated at the right hand of the Father interceding (*praying*) for you. He intercedes (*prays*) for you. He is your...our Lord, Savior, Redeemer, Deliverer and Healer.

A. COMPLETE PACKAGE...COMPLETED WORK

In reading of the atonement process of the Old Testament, we gain a better understanding of the scope and intricacy of Christ's role as High Priest and Sacrifice; empowering us to better appreciate Him, and the covenant He represents and makes available to us. The best that could be achieved from the Old Testament atoning process was being presentable before God. However, it did nothing for the conscience and heart or inner man. There was no venue or present hope of being completely released or absolved of sin. Until Jesus!

Hebrews 9:15-26 *Amplified Bible*
[15] [Christ, the Messiah] is therefore the Negotiator and Mediator of an [entirely] new agreement (testament, covenant), so that those who are called and offered it may receive the fulfillment of the promised everlasting inheritance--since a death has taken place which rescues and delivers and redeems them

71

from the transgressions committed under the [old] first agreement.

[16] For where there is a [last] will and testament involved, the death of the one who made it must be established,

[17] For a will and testament is valid and takes effect only at death, since it has no force or legal power as long as the one who made it is alive.

[18] So even the [old] first covenant (God's will) was not inaugurated and ratified and put in force without the shedding of blood.

[19] For when every command of the Law had been read out by Moses to all the people, he took the blood of slain calves and goats, together with water and scarlet wool and with a bunch of hyssop, and sprinkled both the Book (the roll of the Law and covenant) itself and all the people,

[20] Saying these words: This is the blood that seals and ratifies the agreement (the testament, the covenant) which God commanded [me to deliver to] you.

[21] And in the same way he sprinkled with the blood both the tabernacle and all the [sacred] vessels and appliances used in [divine] worship.

[22] [In fact] under the Law almost everything is purified by means of blood, and without the shedding of blood there is neither release from sin and its guilt nor the remission of the due and merited punishment for sins.

[23] By such means, therefore, it was necessary for the [earthly] copies of the heavenly things to be purified, but the actual heavenly things themselves [required far] better and nobler sacrifices than these.

[24] For Christ (the Messiah) has not entered into a sanctuary made with [human] hands, only a copy and pattern and type of the true one, but [He has entered] into heaven itself, now to appear in the [very] presence of God on our behalf.

[25] Nor did He [enter into the heavenly sanctuary to] offer Himself regularly again and again, as the high priest enters the [Holy of] Holies every year with blood not his own.

[26] For then would He often have had to suffer [over and over again] since the foundation of the world. But as it now is, He has once for all at the consummation and close of the ages appeared to put away and abolish sin by His sacrifice [of Himself].

(Emphasis added – v. 15)

With Jesus as our High Priest *and* the great Sacrificial Sin Offering for us, we have a better covenant. The Old Covenant (*Testament*) was only a foreshadow of what was to come – pointing out the dire need for the promised Messiah, Jesus Christ. He was not only the perfect plan of redemption and reconciliation, but also the fulfillment of that plan: Salvation.

Relationship with the Father is available to us through Salvation by Jesus. He is our way of divine restoration and reconciliation into union with the Father. We can partake of the many blessings, which include fellowship with Him. Because of the finished work of Jesus Christ we can go to the Father directly to give thanks, praise, worship, pray, and make our petitions known to Him. We can now also go directly to the Father to repent – asking His forgiveness; and His assistance in turning away from ungodly behavior. The Lord reassures us of His forgiveness unto us.

1 John 1:9
If we confess our sins, He is faithful and just to forgive us our sins, and to cleanse us from all unrighteousness.
This is not a license or permission to sin but rather a statement of our special covenant with Him, which is not to be taken lightly or for granted.

Some denominations and religions believe that a middleman or mediator of flesh and blood is necessary to present petitions and requests for forgiveness to the Father; however, Scripture proves this is not the case. The only Mediator necessary and fully qualified is Jesus Christ.

Hebrews 7:25
Wherefore He is able also to save them to the uttermost that come unto God by Him, seeing He ever liveth to make intercession for them.

Romans 8:34
Who is he that condemneth? It is Christ that died, yea rather, that is risen again, who is even at the right hand of God, who also maketh intercession for us.

Jesus Himself intercedes for us...He prays for us...He prays for <u>you</u>.

Thank God for the ultimate Sacrifice. **Christ made the perfect, once and for all – for all time and all people – sacrifice, which obtains full forgiveness of sins and thus does away with any need for further sacrifices.** What the sacrifices of the Old Testament pointed to but could not fulfill was achieved, completed: "it is FINISHED" – through the death, burial, resurrection and ascension of Jesus Christ, that magnificent High Priest and perfect Offering. With Jesus having satisfied *all* roles and requirements for us for remission of sin, we are redeemed and justified.

"Justified" as in: shown to be true, right; free from blame, declared innocent or guiltless, absolved, acquitted, defended

Picture a courtroom scene.

> Participants:
> Judge – The Lord God Almighty
> Defense Attorney – Jesus Christ
> Prosecutor – satan/the devil/the adversary
> Defendant – New Creature in Christ, (insert your name here)

When the devil, attempts to accuse New Creatures in Christ to the Court, and recreate a rap sheet on us, listing any offenses/charges/shortcomings, regardless of what they may be, the Blood of Jesus declares, "**Not guilty!**" *("re-create," because it has been expunged)*

Jesus proclaims, "**I have already paid the penalty with My own Blood; and the sentence and all charges have been removed and are as though they never occurred.**"

As a result, in satan's attempts to bring up our past to the Lord, he is actually lying as these things no longer exist, rendering his claims against us null and void. The offense and evidence have been washed away by the Blood of Christ. The devil no longer has a leg to stand on concerning those old things against us. More importantly, the Lord remembers these things no more; we are justified, forgiven, made true and right. Now that is something to shout about...Hallelujah!

Psalm 103:12
    As far as the east is from the west, so far hath He removed our transgressions from us.

Hebrews 8:12
    For I will be merciful to their unrighteousness, and their sins and their iniquities will I remember no more.

Having this understanding of your justification through Christ, and as the Lord has forgiven and forgotten, you must also let them go, remembering them no more. You must forgive yourself, as the Lord has forgiven you; and ask the Lord to assist you in seeing yourself as He sees you...His New Creature in Christ.

2 Corinthians 5:17
Therefore if any man be in Christ, he is a new creature: old things are past away; behold all things are become new.

With all this in mind, know that whatever sin or error you may have committed in the past, is just that..."PAST". Once it has been washed by the Blood of the Lamb, Jesus Christ, at Salvation *(accepting and confessing Him as Lord and Savior)*; and thereafter by immediately repenting for whatever subsequent offenses are committed, it is as if those things never occurred.

Repenting is more than flippantly saying, "Sorry." It is sincerely asking God's forgiveness *AND* setting your heart to turn away from those things – sins, habits, attitudes, behaviors. Through Salvation and repentance you are then able and are to accomplish everything the Lord has established and purposed for you.

There may be consequences that must be resolved – *for example: paying alimony/child support along with arrears; repairing relationships, admitting the truth to someone* – however, because of Christ you can go right in to the Father and ask Him for His plan and instruction on making amends, along with the courage and means to follow through. You are not to attempt to do anything or make any decision on your own; but trusting Him to have and reveal the course of action to take.

The only decision you are ever to immediately make; the only thing you can ever know to do without second-thought or hesitation, is to go to the Lord, your Father, your Counselor for instruction and then implement as He leads.

Past and forgiven sins and iniquities are no longer a hindrance to your fellowship with the Lord, your walk or service in Him; for they have been washed clean away, removed from you.

Oh, the Blood of Jesus! Oh, the love of the Father, Son, and Holy Spirit!

Now you declare aloud: **Hallelujah! I am SAVED! I am forgiven! Hallelujah!**

(If you are not yet born again or have strayed away from the Lord God and desire to return, see Section Seven of this book.)

Remember, God is a covenant God; covenant meaning agreement. The shed Blood of Jesus Christ is the binding force of our covenant with God, the Father. In this, think of it as the ink of God's signature. Through the completed process of the sacrificial offering of and by Jesus Christ – His death, burial, resurrection and ascension – this covenant of Salvation for mankind is established, secured and made available.

Your acceptance of the redeeming action of Jesus Christ seals your personal agreement in God and transitions you into a position of having access to Him and becoming entitled to ALL He is – His nature, character, His being.

At the point of Salvation you become a "New Creature" having a covenant with the Lord. This agreement affords you many benefits, which are available to you immediately. Praise Jesus!

B. HIS NAMES AND CHARACTERISTICS

Getting acquainted with Jesus also includes knowing His Names. Just as we saw that our Father, God has Names, which have great meaning describing His nature and characteristics, His Son, Jesus Christ has Names, which tell who and all He is; and that all He is, He is for you.

Generally speaking, people say the name of God's Son, Jesus Christ, as though His first name is "Jesus" and His last name is "Christ".

The truth is:
<u>Jesus</u> = Jehovah-saves; to be open, wide or free; avenging; defend; deliver(er); help; preserve; rescue; bring salvation; victory[3]

<u>Christ</u> = Anointed; Messiah; consecrate to an office; furnish what is needed[3]

Knowing and understanding the many other Names of Jesus, grounds us in the truth of who He is as well as sets a foundation of who we are because of and in Him. We become confident that we have authority and are successful in taking dominion over the enemy and his forces because we are aware of the depth and power of the Name of Jesus. "In the Name of Jesus" becomes more than a phrase tacked on to our prayers, confessions and declarations. It is the power of attorney appropriated to us by God Himself to accomplish His will here in the earth and live victoriously.

Here are some other Names of Jesus:

<u>Advocate, the Righteous</u>
1 John 2:1
My little children, these things write I unto you, that ye sin not. And if any man sin, we have an advocate with the Father, Jesus Christ the righteous…

Alpha and Omega, the Almighty
Revelation 1:8
I am Alpha and Omega, the beginning and the ending, saith the Lord, which is, and which was, and which is to come, the Almighty.

Begotten Son of God
John 3:16
For God so loved the world, that He gave His only begotten Son, that whosoever believeth in Him should not perish, but have everlasting life.

Bread of Life
John 6:48
I am that bread of life.

Chief Cornerstone
Ephesians 2:19-21
[19] Now therefore ye are no more strangers and foreigners, but fellow citizens with the saints, and of the household of God;

[20] And are built upon the foundation of the apostles and prophets, Jesus Christ Himself being the Chief Corner Stone;

[21] In Whom all the building fitly framed together groweth unto an holy temple in the Lord

Emmanuel – God with us
Matthew 1:23
Behold, a virgin shall be with child, and shall bring forth a Son, and they shall call His name Emmanuel, which being interpreted is, God with us.

Great High Priest
Hebrews 4:14
Seeing then that we have a Great High Priest, that is passed into the heavens, Jesus the Son of God, let us hold fast our profession.

Great Shepherd
Hebrews 13:20
Now the God of Peace, that brought again from the dead our Lord Jesus, that Great Shepherd of the sheep, through the blood of the everlasting covenant…

Judge of Quick and Dead
Acts 10:42
And He commanded us to preach unto the people, and to testify that it is He which was ordained of God to be the Judge of Quick and Dead.

King of Kings, Lord of Lords
1 Timothy 6:15
Which in His times He shall shew, who is the blessed and only Potentate, the King of kings, and Lord of lords…

Revelation 19:16
And He hath on His vesture and on His thigh a name written, KING OF KINGS, AND LORD OF LORDS.

Lamb of God
John 1:29
The next day John seeth Jesus coming unto him, and saith, Behold the Lamb of God, which taketh away the sin of the world.

Light of the World
John 9:5

As long as I am in the world, I am the Light of the World.

Lion of the Tribe of Judah
Revelation 5:5

And one of the elders saith unto me, Weep not: behold, the Lion of the tribe of Judah, the Root of David, hath prevailed to open the book, and to lose the seven seals thereof.

Messiah, the Christ
John 1:41

He first findeth his own brother Simon, and saith unto him, We have found the Messiah, which is, being interpreted, the Christ.

The Root and Offspring of David, Bright and Morning Star
Revelation 22:16

I Jesus have sent mine angel to testify unto you these things in the churches. I am the Root and the Offspring of David, and the Bright and Morning Star.

Servant of God
Isaiah 42:1

Behold My Servant, whom I uphold; mine elect, in Whom My soul delighteth; I have put My Spirit upon Him: He shall bring forth judgment to the Gentiles.

Savior and Hope
1 Timothy 1:1

Paul, an apostle of Jesus Christ by the commandment of God our Saviour, and Lord Jesus Christ, which is our Hope...

Son of God
John 20:31
But these are written, that ye might believe that Jesus is the Christ, the Son of God; and that believing ye might have life through his name.

Son of Man
Matthew 24:30
And then shall appear the sign of the Son of Man in heaven: and then shall all the tribes of the earth mourn, and they shall see the Son of Man coming in the clouds of heaven with power and great glory.

Son of the Blessed
Mark 14:61-62
61 But He held His peace, and answered nothing. Again the high priest asked Him, and said unto Him, Art thou the Christ, the Son of the Blessed?

62 And Jesus said, I am: and ye shall see the Son of Man sitting on the right hand of Power, and coming in the clouds of heaven.

Spiritual Rock
1 Corinthians 10:4
And did all drink the same spiritual drink: for they drank of that Spiritual Rock that followed them: and that Rock was Christ.

The Way, the Truth and the Life
John 14:6
Jesus saith unto him, I am the Way, the Truth, and the Life: no man cometh unto the Father, but by Me.

Wonderful, Counselor, Mighty God, Everlasting Father, Prince of Peace
Isaiah 9:6
For unto us a Child is born, unto us a Son is given: and the government shall be upon His shoulder: and His name shall be called Wonderful, Counselor, The mighty God, The everlasting Father, The Prince of Peace.

The Word, Lord of All
Acts 10:36
The Word which God sent unto the children of Israel, preaching peace by Jesus Christ: (He is Lord of all:)

REFLECTIONS

This concept of knowing and understanding the Names of Jesus is not to bewilder us, but to build our conviction in Him through the awareness of the fullness of Him and diffuse all manner of despair. Be quite assured that the Name of JESUS is so full of Light that when called out in the time of trouble or when sealing a prayer, all darkness must succumb to Its power. In that one Name alone, know that you have victory!

CHAPTER V

SPECIAL MESSAGE

<u>S</u>PECIAL <u>M</u>ESSAGE

When the Lord initially put this teaching on my heart, I asked Him what He wanted us to receive, what particular thing He wanted to divulge to us. Here is His response:

I AM real; I AM alive.
I love you so much that I went in before the Father as <u>THE</u> High Priest and <u>THE</u> Offering. As "High Priest" it was I who went in and spread <u>My</u> own Blood on the mercy seat for you; as "Offering" it was <u>My</u> Blood, for there was none more powerful – strong enough, anointed enough to achieve and accomplish the task.

I did it for you. I did it for Us – the Godhead. The Father, We, required it so you could come in unto Us. In this you are made, set free. In this you are more than a conqueror; only believe!

You struggle so, when you need not. All things are under My feet and as I am in you by Our precious Holy Spirit, they are under your feet also. Walk in the liberty provided by Me. Live, walk, breathe in the victory established by Me.

Fellowship with Us. Come, sit at the table prepared, set, established for you – set with: love, peace, joy, increase, strength, provision of every type, abundance, counsel of: answers, direction and encouragement and yes, correction– these are all awaiting you at the table.

Our Word is for you; every promise; every blessing is for you, in Me.

Come and know My love for you. Come and partake. Come and enjoy. Set your heart, determine in your heart to fellowship with Us – as a lifestyle. All I have done enables you to do so.

Come. Come. Come.

*This "come" is an invitation, but also a **command**.*

*You are Mine, I paid the price for you. I see you contending in things that are already defeated and in which you already have the victory. **STOP**...and come in unto Me, where you will:*

- *See yourself as I see you*
- *See who you are by Me*
- *See the situations and circumstances as I see them...in victory*
- *Understand your position in Me*
- *Understand your position because of Me*
- *Understand what I have done for you...as High Priest and Offering.*

Come. Come. Come!
Amen.

SECTION THREE

THE FULFILLMENT

FOUNDATION SCRIPTURE:
Romans 10:4 *Amplified Bible*
For Christ is the end of the Law [the limit at which it ceases to be, for the Law leads up to Him Who is the fulfillment of its types, and in Him the purpose which it was designed to accomplish is fulfilled. That is, the purpose of the Law is fulfilled in Him] as the means of righteousness (right relationship to God) for everyone who trusts in and adheres to and relies on Him.

INTRODUCTION
We must understand that our standing with God as New Creatures involves the fulfillment through Jesus Christ of what the Old Testament alluded to; and thus providing the new and better covenant to mankind. This sets the foundation for our newness with God – restored sonship, benefits realized, and promises satisfied. Having the right foundation, we come to know that we do not have to be subject to the wiles of the enemy or his schemes. We learn that our success and victory are not dependent on anything he allows.

To reinforce our foundation regarding the atoning redemptive work of Christ and better appreciate this completed work, let's compare the Old Testament annual observance and the one time New Testament fulfillment by Him.

CHAPTER I

THE OLD TESTAMENT DAY OF ATONEMENT

THE OLD TESTAMENT DAY OF ATONEMENT

The Day of Atonement, "Yom Kippur," was and remains the holiest day of the Jewish year and observances. It is a solemn assembly of the people to fast and humble themselves before the Lord; a time to reflect on the seriousness of sin and the implications of becoming right with Him by the covering of their sins.

"Atonement" stems from the need to make restitution or payment *("kopher" – a price for ransom of a life[4])* for sin. This payment was necessary to stem off the justly due wrath of God for the sin committed. The annual observance of atonement was to appease the penalty for sin. This all-encompassing sacrifice allowed for the children of Israel to sustain a righted position with their Lord Jehovah. This was a type of salvation, which pointed to the ultimate Salvation acquired by and through the final, once and for all sacrifice of Jesus Christ.

Under the Old Covenant, the high priest prepared himself for the annual observance of the Day of Atonement according to the instruction of the Lord, which included a sin offering for himself and his own house. The sin offering required blood for legitimacy and fulfillment. *(Hebrews 9:22)* After atoning for himself he conducted the ceremonial sacrifice for the people. Two goats without spot or blemish were selected for the proceedings.

Leviticus 16:8-10

8 And Aaron shall cast lots upon the two goats; one lot for the LORD, and the other lot for the scapegoat.

9 And Aaron shall bring the goat upon which the LORD's lot fell, and offer him for a sin offering.

10 But the goat, on which the lot fell to be the scapegoat, shall be presented alive before the LORD, to make an atonement with him, and to let him go for a scapegoat into the wilderness.

Designation between the goats was made by casting lots - one goat was for the sin offering; and the other goat was used as the scapegoat. *(To choose by lot or to "cast lots" refers to the practice of throwing lots – similar to drawing/pulling straws or tossing a coin – allowing the result to determine a decision, however the determination of the lot was considered the Divine decision, being caused by God Himself.)* The goat selected for the sin offering was killed and its blood spread as required.

Leviticus 16:20-22

20 And when he hath made an end of reconciling the holy place, and the tabernacle of the congregation, and the altar, he shall bring the live goat:

21 And Aaron shall lay both his hands upon the head of the live goat, and confess over him all the iniquities of the children of Israel, and all their transgressions in all their sins, putting them upon the head of the goat, and shall send him away by the hand of a fit man into the wilderness:

22 And the goat shall bear upon him all their iniquities unto a land not inhabited: and he shall let go the goat in the wilderness.

After making the sin offering using the first goat, the high priest then laid his hands on the head of the second goat – the scapegoat. This action represented the transfer of all the sins of the people onto the animal. The scapegoat or Goat of Departure is so called because it ceremonially took on and carried away the iniquities of the people. The goat driven out into the wilderness only eased their consciences of the guilt associated with the sin. The term scapegoat is still used today to describe a person who takes the blame for someone else's wrongdoing.

The scapegoat of the Old Testament points to Jesus, the supreme Scapegoat, as He bore the sins for mankind.

CHAPTER II

THE NEW TESTAMENT COVENANT OF REDEMPTION

THE NEW TESTAMENT COVENANT OF REDEMPTION

Hebrews 10:1-4
¹ For the law having a shadow of good things to come, and not the very image of the things, can never with those sacrifices which they offered year by year continually make the comers thereunto perfect.

² For then would they not have ceased to be offered? because that the worshippers once purged should have had no more conscience of sins.

³ But in those sacrifices there is a remembrance again made of sins every year.

⁴ For it is not possible that the blood of bulls and of goats should take away sins.

The blood of animals could not possibly achieve what the powerful Blood of Jesus accomplished – the complete forgiveness and removal of sins; complete as in lacking no parts, being thorough, perfect, total – redeeming man.

Hebrews 10:5-9
⁵ Wherefore when He cometh into the world, He saith, Sacrifice and offering Thou wouldest not, but a body hast Thou prepared Me:

⁶ In burnt offerings and sacrifices for sin Thou hast had no pleasure.

⁷ Then said I, Lo, I come (in the volume of the book it is written of Me,) to do Thy will, O God.

⁸ Above when He said, Sacrifice and offering and burnt offerings and offering for sin Thou wouldest not, neither hadst pleasure therein; which are offered by the law;

⁹ Then said He, Lo, I come to do Thy will, O God. He taketh away the first, that He may establish the second.

Let's seriously ponder the conversation between Jesus and the Lord as portrayed in this text:

> "Father, You have not found any pleasure in burnt offerings and sacrifices. There is no complete satisfaction for You in these. The people are still limited in relationship and fellowship with You because the sin is still there. Let Me take care of this as it is written of Me to do."

Hebrews 2:17
Wherefore in all things it behoved Him to be made like unto His brethren, that He might be a merciful and faithful High Priest in things pertaining to God, to make reconciliation for the sins of the people.

Hebrews 10:10-18
¹⁰ By the which will we are sanctified through the offering of the body of Jesus Christ once for all.

¹¹ And every priest standeth daily ministering and offering oftentimes the same sacrifices, which can never take away sins:

¹² But this Man, after He had offered one sacrifice for sins for ever, sat down on the right hand of God;

¹³ From henceforth expecting till His enemies be made His footstool.

¹⁴ For by one offering He hath perfected for ever them that are sanctified.

¹⁵ Whereof the Holy Ghost also is a witness to us: for after that He had said before,

¹⁶ This is the covenant that I will make with them after those days, saith the Lord, I will put my laws into their hearts, and in their minds will I write them;

¹⁷ And their sins and iniquities will I remember no more.

¹⁸ Now where remission of these is, there is no more offering for sin.

Because of the great sacrifice of Christ there is no further need for the blood of animals to atone for sin, nor for a scapegoat to carry away the guilt. Jesus took every sin – past, present and future – and the guilt of them upon Himself, and made Salvation available to all mankind.

Think of Salvation as a Divine Transaction:
- Sin incurring a cost, a penalty too costly for us to pay ourselves

- Jesus came to pay the high price of the penalty for us; giving His life – shedding and using His own blood as the currency

- The debt is paid in full

As a result, we are personally able to receive the Lord and from Him directly; along with the assurance that He does not even remember our sins and iniquities *(the residue)* of them. The Salvation transaction is represented in the actions that occurred when Jesus was crucified; on what is commonly referred to as "Good Friday."

The cross on that day, which I will refer to as "Friday Cross" or "Pre-Resurrection Cross," is the cross of crucifixion and sacrifice unto death where the beaten, sin-ridden, guilt-riddled body of Jesus hung. It is here where He "gave up the ghost" *(His life)*; dying for us so we could live.

Oh, but it did not end there...for He is alive!

Matthew 28:5-6
[5] And the angel answered and said unto the women, Fear not ye: for I know that ye seek Jesus, which was crucified.

[6] He is not here: for He is risen; as He said. Come, see the place where the Lord lay.

Mark 8:31
And He (Jesus) began to teach them, that the Son of Man must suffer many things, and be rejected of the elders, and of the chief priests, and scribes, and be killed, and after three days rise again.

Three days later *(Sunday – Easter/Resurrection Sunday)* came the resurrection, when Jesus rose from the dead, having conquered death.

Revelation 1:18
I am He that liveth, and was dead; behold, I am alive for evermore, Amen; and have the keys of hell and of death.

The "Friday Cross" has been replaced with the "Sunday Cross," the Cross of Resurrection. Although in actuality there was only one cross, its appearance was changed by the resurrection power of God. The body of Jesus no longer hangs there, it is no longer in the grave; and all sin, along with all guilt and penalty, which He bore while nailed to that cross are gone as well. Hallelujah! He not only rose from the dead *(resurrection)*, but also returned to heaven *(ascension)*. Glory to God!

(Many may argue which day of the week, week of the month, month of the year this monumental event occurred; getting lost in semantics, distracted by vain discussions, and missing the magnitude of the event: Salvation, forgiveness for sin, redemption from the penalty of sin, restoration to relationship with the Lord as His sons and daughters, eternal life with God – victory for today and heaven as our future. The Bible even tells us to avoid foolish questions and contention. (Titus 3:9)

There is good reason and purpose for accurate history and corresponding dates, but never to the detriment of the glory of the Lord.)

The solemn assembly for atonement by the children of Israel of the Old Testament pointed to what was to come. Jesus is the fulfillment of what they could only hope to achieve: total reconciliation to God. To only think of Him as still on the cross, is to think of Him as defeated, never having achieved victory for us. Jesus, having risen from the dead, is now seated at the right hand of the Father interceding for us, New Creatures in Christ. Through His victory over sin and death we also have victory. In Christ, we are fully absolved from <u>all</u> penalty of sin.

CHAPTER III

ATONEMENT, SALVATION COMPARISON

ATONEMENT, SALVATION COMPARISON

The Levitical observance sets the scene for the greater and perfect Sacrifice that was yet to come, Jesus Christ. Old Testament provides hope; hope for a sure Salvation. New Testament presents the manifestation, the delivery of what was promised; that sure Salvation.

Let's compare:

Old Testament	New Testament
Atonement	Salvation
Foreshadow	Fulfillment
Thing	Person
Blood – animal	Blood – Jesus Christ
Annual	Once, for all time and all people
Cleanse/wipe/cover/appease	Remove/ransom price/escape death penalty

Today, the process of obtaining salvation and forgiveness for sin is simply Romans 10:9...

> That if thou shalt confess with thy mouth the Lord Jesus, and shalt believe in thine heart that God hath raised Him from the dead, thou shalt be saved.

"Simply," as in untainted, pure and concise...just speak the Word and believe in your heart.

Romans 10:10 explains...
For with the heart man believeth unto righteousness; and with the mouth confession is made unto salvation.

Acts 16:31
And they said, Believe on the Lord Jesus Christ, and thou shalt be saved, and thy house.

As a result:
2 Corinthians 5:17

Therefore if any man be in Christ, he is a new creature: old things are passed away; behold, all things are become new.

2 Corinthians 3:16-18 *Amplified Bible*
[16] But whenever a person turns [in repentance] to the Lord, the veil is stripped off and taken away.

[17] Now the Lord is the Spirit, and where the Spirit of the Lord is, there is liberty (emancipation from bondage, freedom).

[18] And all of us, as with unveiled face, [because we] continued to behold [in the Word of God] as in a mirror the glory of the Lord, are constantly being transfigured into His very own image in ever increasing splendor and from one degree of glory to another; [for this comes] from the Lord [Who is] the Spirit.

REFLECTIONS

John 8:36
If the Son therefore shall make you free, ye shall be free indeed.

The fulfillment or completion of the process of redemption by Jesus Christ totally sets us free. All separation between God and us is removed. We are now able to have a relationship with the Lord directly.

Side note:
Forgiveness for any subsequent sins, those committed after your initial confession unto Salvation, is addressed in 1 John 1:9…

> If we confess our sins, He is faithful and just to forgive us our sins, and to cleanse us of all unrighteousness.

We can and are to go directly to God, the Father, in the Name of Jesus Christ and confess the offense to Him. You become engaged in God's awaiting love and forgiveness when you come to Him with a sincere heart of repentance – turning away from sinful behavior, actions and lifestyle, and to God and holiness *(His ways)*. Jesus has already made and declared us forgiven, having shed His own blood for all sin – past, present and future. However, every person is responsible for accepting His forgiveness and repenting.

Although God has made all necessary provision for us…for you…to be partakers of the liberty Jesus offers, each person must choose to accept what He has made available. Everyone must make his/her own decision to make Jesus Christ, the Son of God, his/her personal Lord and Savior.

(If you have not yet prayed for Jesus to come into your heart, please refer to the Prayer of Salvation in the back of this book; join the family of God and receive full remission of your sins, and restoration of fellowship with the Father.)

GETTING ACQUAINTED WITH HOLY SPIRIT

<u>FOUNDATION SCRIPTURE:</u>
John 14:17
Even the Spirit of truth; whom the world cannot receive, because it seeth Him not, neither knoweth Him: but ye know Him; for He dwelleth with you, and shall be in you.

<u>INTRODUCTION</u>
There is no place where God is not: not present...not aware...not God Almighty. God's presence is in the earth, in the universe and in us by/through His Spirit.

- He is all-knowing – <u>omniscient</u>

- He is ever-present, everywhere – <u>omnipresent</u>

- He is all-powerful, invincible, unstoppable, supreme – <u>omnipotent</u>

John 14:18
I will not leave you comfortless: I will come to you.

In Jesus' promise of sending the Comforter upon His own leaving, He states, "I will come to you." This is not a contradiction, but a confirmation of the three Persons of the Godhead – Father, Son and Holy Spirit. *(1 John 5:7; John 1:14)*

God sent of Himself to us in two ways:

- By the flesh: Jesus Christ

- By the Spirit: Holy Spirit, *(also referred to as the Holy Ghost)*

John 16:7
Nevertheless I tell you the truth; It is expedient for you that I go away: for if I go not away, the Comforter will not come unto you; but if I depart, I will send Him unto you.

CHAPTER I

ENTER HOLY SPIRIT

<u>ENTER HOLY SPIRIT</u>

Who is He, this Holy Spirit?

- He is a Person of the Godhead – Father, Son and Holy Spirit/Ghost.

- He is the breath of God – the life-giving breath of God.

- He is the Administrator of the Godhead – counseling us; revealing the things of the Godhead; and causing their operation in the earth and through us.

- He brings light to otherwise dark situations and circumstances – revealing the depth of the Word of God; interpreting and teaching It to provide answers, instruction, direction, comfort, joy and peace.

- He causes us to triumph – helping us; enduing us with the power and anointing of Himself, God.

Luke 3:16
John (the Baptist) answered, saying unto them all, I indeed baptize you with water; but One mightier than I cometh, the latchet of Whose shoes I am not worthy to unloose: He shall baptize you with the Holy Ghost and with fire:

John 7:38-39
[38] He that believeth on me, as the scripture hath said, out of his belly shall flow rivers of living water.

[39] (But this spake He of the Spirit, which they that believe on Him should receive: for the Holy Ghost was not yet given; because that Jesus was not yet glorified.)

John 14:17
Even the Spirit of truth; whom the world cannot receive, because it seeth Him not, neither knoweth Him: but ye know Him; for He dwelleth with you, and shall be in you

John 20:22
And when He had said this, He breathed on them, and saith unto them, Receive ye the Holy Ghost...

When we accept and confess Jesus Christ as our personal Lord and Savior, the Lord takes up residence in us by way of the Holy Spirit. It is the immediate New Covenant encounter between the Lord and the believer. This is the inbreathed breath of God or the "indwelling" breath of God, which is by His Holy Spirit.

Genesis 2:7
And the LORD God formed man of the dust of the ground, and breathed into his nostrils the breath of life; and man became a living soul.

The creation of the first man came alive when God breathed Himself – the Spirit of Life – into what was formed of the dust of the ground. His breath – the wind, the air – of Him, brought the formed mound of dust to life.

John 20:19-22
[19] Then the same day at evening, being the first day of the week, when the doors were shut where the disciples were assembled for fear of the Jews, came Jesus and stood in the midst, and saith unto them, Peace be unto you.

²⁰ And when He had so said, He shewed unto them His hands and His side. Then were the disciples glad, when they saw the Lord.

²¹ Then said Jesus to them again, Peace be unto you: as My Father hath sent Me, even so send I you.

²² And when He had said this, He breathed on them, and saith unto them, Receive ye the Holy Ghost...

Just as life came into that first newly created man – by the breath, the Spirit of God; so does new life come into the saved, New Creation man – by the breath, the Holy Spirit of God, the Spirit of Life...that is NEW LIFE. This breath of new life occurs at Salvation

Romans 10:9
If you confess with your mouth the Lord Jesus and believe in your heart that God has raised Him from the dead, you will be saved.

In confessing with your mouth, Jesus as Lord, and believing in your heart that God raised Him from the dead, you enter into "New Life" status. You become a New Creature or Creation of His. At this point, the life-giving breath of the Lord through Jesus, (who conquered all things evil – including sin and death), fills/indwells you...giving you newness of life...a triumphant life. Glory to the Most High God!

As magnificent and powerful as this is, the indwelling was not the completed fulfillment of the promise of another Comforter. There is more. There is also the "gift," or "baptism" of the Holy Ghost, which is the added "oomph" *(power)* needed to live and serve Him victoriously. This baptism of the Holy Spirit is in addition to receiving the Holy Spirit at Salvation. *(Acts 8:12-17)*

Acts 8:14-16

¹⁴ Now when the apostles which were at Jerusalem heard that Samaria had received the word of God, they sent unto them Peter and John:

¹⁵ Who, when they were come down, prayed for them, that they might receive the Holy Ghost:

¹⁶ (For as yet he was fallen upon none of them: only they were baptized in the name of the Lord Jesus.)

The Biblical foundational events supporting the two components of the complete manifestation of the Holy Ghost are:

- Indwelling – Resurrection Sunday: Jesus rose from the dead; occurs in us at Salvation

- Baptism – Pentecost: outpouring of the Spirit; occurs in us as we desire to be filled with His power from on high and pray to the Lord to receive it

The baptism of the Holy Spirit is an operation of the Spirit of God. It is a distinct occurrence of application in the life of the New Creature in Christ; with the work of regenerating *(renewal)* and consecrating *(setting apart)* of the heart having been completed at Salvation.

Luke 24:49-53

⁴⁹ And, behold, I send the promise of my Father upon you: but tarry ye in the city of Jerusalem, until ye be endued with power from on high.

⁵⁰ And He led them out as far as to Bethany, and He lifted up his hands, and blessed them.

⁵¹ And it came to pass, while He blessed them, He was parted from them, and carried up into heaven.

⁵² And they worshipped Him, and returned to Jerusalem with great joy:

⁵³ And were continually in the temple, praising and blessing God. Amen.

We bless and please God when we worship, praise and give thanks to Him. These also set the atmosphere for God to manifest Himself to us by His Holy Spirit. Yes, the Lord is always with us, never leaving or forsaking us, but when we spend intentional time praising and worshiping Him the atmosphere shifts, the tone changes. Although we do not rely on feelings, our Father will cause us to tangibly experience His presence.

Testimony:
I had joined the weekly Intercessory Prayer Ministry at the church I was attending at that time. It was in the south suburbs and I worked on the north side of Chicago. My original thought, at detecting the tug on my heart to participate in this ministry, was to do it when and as long as I could, for my concern was punctuality. After starting, I discovered it was where and what I was supposed be doing. Then my concern became getting there on time without being frazzled.

As the Lord worked it out, I would arrive 30-45 minutes early and before anyone else. Now let me make it clear, I was not speeding – Chicago rush hour traffic makes speeding impossible. When I arrived at the church I had the sanctuary all to myself – it was awesome. It was as if He was there awaiting my arrival. I would begin praying and blessing the Lord.

One week He put it on my heart to bring a particular CD and player. After a short while, I reached the point where I would ask Him what, if any, music He wanted for the session – sometimes it would be yes and sometimes no. Then I noticed that I had become a "regular." There was no more "if I could." It had become, "This is what I do."

There was another regular, a mother of the church, who commented that she could feel the presence of the Lord when she arrived, and started coming earlier; and we would usher in the manifest presence of the Holy Spirit together. Attendance increased although few were regulars. Many would comment about how they could sense the Lord was there.

The person overseeing the ministry, was actually filling in for someone else, but we knew it was all God appointed. This minister encouraged and coached me; and I grew, all under the sovereign care of the Lord. During these sessions, deliverance and healing occurred for many; and answers, direction and instruction received – for there was nothing hindering, binding or distracting. We had an audience with the King.

This testimony is not to say that *"I alone"* am extra-super-special. But it is an example of what will happen when we...*you also,* "bless the Lord" – setting the atmosphere, preparing the room and our heart for Him. As we do, we will see that He steps in and makes it all flow – we enter into His presence when we praise; there is strength in praise; the blessings come down when we praise: there is definite benefit when we praise and worship the Lord.

With this perspective, is it any wonder the devil, the adversary works so hard to keep us from praising?

Praise and worship are not limited to the church building, sanctuary, or any particular person, position or event. Each and every New Creature in Christ can and should bless the Lord and enter into His presence. We can set things in order for Him to enter in and manifest Himself. I have heard a minister of praise and worship say to the audience, "Give Him something to inhabit." You see, the Lord tells us that He inhabits the praises of His people; He is our praise...He comes: by His Holy Spirit, He comes when we praise. *(Psalm 22:3; Deuteronomy 10:21)*

John 14:16-17

¹⁶ And I will pray the Father, and He shall give you another Comforter, that He may abide with you for ever;

¹⁷ Even the Spirit of truth; whom the world cannot receive, because it seeth Him not, neither knoweth Him: but ye know Him; for He <u>dwelleth with you</u>, and <u>shall be in you</u>.

(Emphasis added – v. 17)

In expressing the promise of another Comforter, Jesus is making a statement to the disciples of the impending divine exchange:

"dwelleth with you" – currently, as Jesus
"shall be in you" – after Jesus' ascension, as the Holy Spirit

John 14:18-21

¹⁸ I will not leave you comfortless: I will come to you.

¹⁹ Yet a little while, and the world seeth Me no more; but ye see Me: because I live, ye shall live also.

²⁰ At that day ye shall know that I am in my Father, and ye in Me, and I in you.

²¹ He that hath My commandments, and keepeth them, He it is that loveth Me: and He that loveth Me shall be loved of My Father, and I will love Him, and will manifest myself to Him.

This promised Comforter ("parakletos" – intercessor, consoler, advocate[3]), is of the same sort after Jesus Christ: everything Jesus is, so is this Comforter. A function or position of the Comforter is "para" – from the Greek word meaning to be near, beside[3].

God promises in Hebrews 13:5, "that He will never leave us, nor forsake us." It is by His precious Holy Spirit that He fulfills this unto us.

CHAPTER II

GIVE HIM THE RIGHT PLACE

<u>GIVE HIM THE RIGHT PLACE</u>

When you give the Holy Ghost the right place in your life you will:

- See the supernatural gifts and manifestations in operation

- Live the life of an overcomer

- See powerful results as you serve the Lord

- Become a greater witness of Him to the world

You may be wondering, "How do I give the Holy Ghost the right place in my life?"

It begins with prayer, a conversation with the Lord to accept the gift of the Holy Ghost.

<u>Sample Prayer</u>

> "Father, I desire and accept Your gift of the Holy Spirit. I not only desire all that You have for me, but I realize I need this additional power from You to live in close fellowship with You and in victory, to serve You and accomplish all You have established for me.
>
> I thank and praise You for this gift of Yourself, the Holy Ghost; in the Name of Jesus Christ. Amen."

Here are a few suggestions for giving Him proper placement in your life:

- Ask Him regularly to cause you not to miss what He has for you – any encounter, blessing or assignment. Be confident that He is with you always, and will always answer, but do not expect Him to come or answer in the same way all the time. Remember, God is quite creative.

- Speak what the Word of God says. Speak God's answer for the matter instead of speaking the problem. Make the petition known, thereafter speak the Word only. For example – you have the sniffles. You should immediately speak the Word, "By the stripes of Jesus, I am healed" *(Isaiah 53:5; 1 Peter 2:24)*; instead of "I'm catching a cold; it's that time of year."

- Adhere to, yes, that would be "OBEY," His prompting and leading, which may come as an impression on your heart or the still small voice, oftentimes referred to as "something told me". Go when He says go. Stop when He says stop.

Testimony:
I attended a wedding in a neighboring state. There were severe thunderstorms all that day. In spite of the weather everything went well; except for the woman knocking people over trying to catch the bouquet – but that is a story for another time.

On my trip home I ran into several detours because of flooding, which led me further away from the expressway and off the course of my directions and map. I stopped for directions, but the main alternate roads were also closed. Then I asked the Lord for help. Immediately I could "perceive" the Holy Spirit directing me with impressions on my heart – "turn left here...go straight...turn right," etc. He led me through fog, dark, and woodsy back roads to my home state, and a familiar main road that led me to an expressway home. I was so calm and had such peace during the adventure that I was surprised.

A few days later I "came across" Isaiah 30:21 Amplified Bible

> *And your ears will hear a word behind you, saying, This is the way; walk in it, when you turn to the right hand and when you turn to the left.*

Glory to God! That's <u>my</u> Holy Ghost!

There have been other times when I was driving and got a little turned around – I never say that I am lost, God knows exactly where I am at all times – and the Holy Spirit will remind me of those words of Isaiah 30:21; and my heart is made clear to receive His direction.

We are not to grieve the Holy Spirit by ignoring His presence, voice or guiding. Consistently resisting Him will cause Him to back off and let you do things your own way. Although the Lord will never leave or forsake us; holding to this mode of operation will cause you to step out from under His "umbrella" of grace and protection.

Repentance will bring you back in right position, but it is quite foolish and dangerous to insult the Holy Spirit and find yourself truly flying solo. There is no condemnation here; know that God loves you with an everlasting love and will forgive you when you return to Him with a sincere heart and confess your sins. Amen.

CHAPTER III

GENUINE, COMPLETE VICTORY

GENUINE, COMPLETE VICTORY

Only by the Holy Spirit is the New Creature able to live in genuine and complete victory. Our spirit may be willing but, as Jesus states, the flesh is weak. *(Matthew 26:41)* As much as we may desire to do the right thing, go the right way, stay away from what is wrong; and as much as we may try, our attempts are futile without the empowering assistance of the Holy Spirit. We may have some successes, but they will not last and the toil it takes to acquire them is not how the Lord designed success to be or for us to live.

This is not to say all will be easy; work is required of us. However, when we trust, rely on and adhere to the Holy Spirit we will have genuine, complete victory.

Romans 7:18-8:2

[18] For I know that in me (that is, in my flesh,) dwelleth no good thing: for to will is present with me; but how to perform that which is good I find not.

[19] For the good that I would I do not: but the evil which I would not, that I do.

[20] Now if I do that I would not, it is no more I that do it, but sin that dwelleth in me.

[21] I find then a law, that, when I would do good, evil is present with me.

[22] For I delight in the law of God after the inward man:

²³ But I see another law in my members, warring against the law of my mind, and bringing me into captivity to the law of sin which is in my members.

²⁴ O wretched man that I am! who shall deliver me from the body of this death?

²⁵ I thank God through Jesus Christ our Lord. So then with the mind I myself serve the law of God; but with the flesh the law of sin.

⁸⁺¹ There is therefore now no condemnation to them which are in Christ Jesus, who walk not after the flesh, but after the Spirit.

² For the law of the Spirit of life in Christ Jesus hath made me free from the law of sin and death.

This is a mouthful, and may seem a bit confusing. Paul is *not* saying, "I'll just think about doing the right things and serve the Lord while I do my own thing." He *is* making the point that there are desires of the flesh that do not line up with the ways of the Lord that work to oppose what we know to be right.

With the Holy Spirit, our Helper, we can have this testimony:

> "I know what is right, and I desire to do that. My flesh may fight against my doing what is right, but I thank my God for the victory I have in and by Christ Jesus. I walk after the Spirit and am no longer a slave to my flesh."

Paul acknowledges that there is no good thing in and of his flesh – ways, desires, works – as the flesh is corrupt, *and* it must be subjected to the things and control of the Spirit of God. We must <u>surrender</u> and <u>submit</u> to God.

- Surrender – give up our own way and take on His

- Submit – obey His commands, even the seemingly small and insignificant things

Romans 6:11-14

[11] Likewise reckon ye also yourselves to be dead indeed unto sin, but alive unto God through Jesus Christ our Lord.

[12] Let not sin therefore reign in your mortal body, that ye should obey it in the lusts thereof.

[13] Neither yield ye your members as instruments of unrighteousness unto sin: but yield yourselves unto God, as those that are alive from the dead, and your members as instruments of righteousness unto God.

[14] For sin shall not have dominion over you: for ye are not under the law, but under grace.

Just as Paul, we also are to understand that our flesh of limitations and challenges no longer has lordship or rule over us. We learn that although our heart is regenerated at Salvation, our mind must be renewed by the Word of God. *(Romans 12:2)*

So we begin reading the Bible. But the devil immediately attempts to put a halt to all the renewing and transforming. He works to make us feel hopeless and helpless, heaping condemnation on us as we read verses such as John 14:15 *Amplified Bible* – "If you [really] love Me, you will keep (obey) My commands."

He will bring up every failed attempt, every misspoken word, and every occurrence of buckling to temptation, throwing accusations our way:

"So you thought you would not do that, go there or say that again."

"If you really loved Him, you would do what is right."

"You're supposed to be a New Creature, but look at you...you're thinking about 'it'...thought you were delivered."

Well, of course it crossed our mind; the devil is shooting the thoughts at us like darts and arrows.

He does all this taunting and accusing to try to stop us from reading on to the next verse, **John 14:16**:

> And I will ask the Father, and He will give you another Comforter (Counselor, Helper, Intercessor, Advocate, Strengthener, and Standby), that He may remain with you forever.
>
> *(Amplified Bible)*

Our Comforter is with us to do what we cannot completely do ourselves. Hallelujah! We do not have to deal with things in our own ability or from our own resolve. Jesus has prayed and God has provided a Helper.

You cannot and do not have to do it in and of yourself. You may find it difficult to impossible...fretting, worrying, and so on. But glory to God, the Holy Spirit, your Helper, gives you strength; empowers you, so you do not have to be overtaken in sin or by the flesh; you have victory in those trials, difficulties and temptations, *AND* He keeps you sane.

In addition, always keep in mind that you also have authority given by Jesus Christ to tell the sender of those crazy thoughts and accusations to get away from you. We are to resist the devil and he will flee. We resist him with the Word of God – reading, meditating and confessing it. And when, perchance you miss it, there is no condemnation from God. Immediately repent, and accept His forgiveness, assistance and deliverance from what caused you to stumble.

Help is provided for us; however, each of us must decide to accept the Helper and the help He offers.

CHAPTER IV

HE USES THE DEPOSITS IN YOU

HE USES THE DEPOSITS IN YOU

The Holy Spirit will use the Word of God deposited in you, pulling it up, reminding you of it, to enable you to use it as the sword/the weapon it is, with perfect precision and timing. When times and struggles of temptation occur, do what Jesus did when tempted in the wilderness – immediately counteract it, shut it down with the Word.

John 14:26
But the Comforter, which is the Holy Ghost, whom the Father will send in My name, He shall teach you all things, and bring all things to your remembrance, whatsoever I have said unto you.

For instance:
Have you ever read a particular Scripture several times over the course of time; heard it spoken at various settings – then one day, you come across that same verse and it is as if a spotlight was beaming on it...the heavens opened up, and new, intense meaning settled in your heart...great depth revealed? You have just experienced a working of the Holy Spirit.

He also brings things to our remembrance...calling up what the Word has said to you, those things that have been deposited in you. In order for this to occur there must be something deposited, something for Him to bring up, something for Him to remind you of – the Word, the faith, the righteous indignation, the determination, all of which come by spending quality time with the Lord.

- <u>Personal study</u> – reading, meditating on the Word, which is God Himself

- <u>Prayer</u> – conversing with the Lord, which includes listening

- <u>Thanksgiving</u> – gives access into His gates

- <u>Praise</u> – the way to enter into His courts

- <u>Worship</u> – focusing on who He is, His power and might, His Names (characteristics)

- <u>Fasting</u> – denying your flesh, letting it know that it is not the boss of you

- <u>BE STILL</u> – hush, get out of His way

And with <u>ALL</u> of these – it is not just about doing it in the church house or corporately as a body...it is PERSONAL. MAKE IT PERSONAL. Making time, spending time...He and you...you and He – is how your confidence, endurance and faith are developed and fortified.

As our Teacher, the Holy Spirit imparts whatever we will ever need to know. He shall provide every necessary instruction. When we adhere to – listen, receive and follow through on – what He says, we are made strong, sure and powerful in Him.

CHAPTER V

HE CAME WITH POWER

He Came With Power

Luke 24:49
And behold, I send the promise of my Father upon you: but tarry ye in the city of Jerusalem, until ye be endued with power from on high.

Acts 1:6-8
6 When they therefore were come together, they asked of Him, saying, Lord, wilt thou at this time restore again the kingdom to Israel?

7 And He said unto them, It is not for you to know the times or the seasons, which the Father hath put in His own power.

8 But ye shall receive power, after that the Holy Ghost is come upon you: and ye shall be witnesses unto Me both in Jerusalem, and in all Judaea, and in Samaria, and unto the uttermost part of the earth.

The word "power" here is translated from the Greek word "dunamis" – defined as force; specifically miraculous power; ability, abundance, might, mighty deed; worker of miracle(s); strength; violence; mighty (wonderful) work[3].

This power enables you to serve the Lord and do the things Jesus did, and even greater. This is the same power that raised Jesus from the dead. Think about it. You have the same power that raised Jesus from the dead living on the inside of you, and made available for your use.

2 Corinthians 4:7-9 *(New International Version)*
⁷ But we have this <u>treasure</u> in <u>jars of clay</u> to show that this all-surpassing power is from God and not from us.

⁸ We are hard pressed on every side, but not crushed; perplexed, but not in despair;

⁹ Persecuted, but not abandoned; struck down, but not destroyed.

(Emphasis added – v. 7)

"Treasure" = Holy Spirit
"Jars of clay" = man, our mortal bodies, and brittle

You have the power to tread on serpents and scorpions and nothing by any means shall hurt you. *(Luke 10:19)* So you can confidently, boldly, courageously go, do and serve according to the Lord's plan for you. Pressure may come, opposition presented and challenges lie in wait, but they *cannot* defeat, crush or destroy you; for God Himself, by the Holy Spirit, is in you, with you, helping you, teaching you and leading you into victory. Hallelujah!

CHAPTER VI

WE ARE NEVER ALONE

<u>WE ARE NEVER ALONE</u>

In knowing the Names, the characteristics of the Holy Spirit, we are made aware of what Help we have available for us and working on our behalf.

Let's explore some of the Names of Holy Spirit.

<u>Administrator of the Godhead</u>
As Administrator, the Holy Spirit reveals and dispenses to us what God has available for His children – divine direction and answers, along with instruction for life application of the things of the Kingdom to which we now belong.

Romans 8:26-27
[26] Likewise the Spirit also helpeth our infirmities: for we know not what we should pray for as we ought: but the Spirit Itself maketh intercession for us with groanings which cannot be uttered.

[27] And He that searcheth the hearts knoweth what is the mind of the Spirit, because He maketh intercession for the saints according to the will of God.

Romans 8:16
The Spirit Itself beareth witness with our spirit, that we are the children of God...

Breath of God
Genesis 2:7
And the LORD God formed man of the dust of the ground, and breathed into his nostrils the breath of life; and man became a living soul.

John 20:22
And when He had said this, He breathed on them, and saith unto them, Receive ye the Holy Ghost...

Comforter
John 14:16
And I will pray the Father, and He shall give you another Comforter, that He may abide with you for ever...

Fire
Luke 3:16
John answered, saying unto them all, I indeed baptize you with water; but one mightier than I cometh, the latchet of whose shoes I am not worthy to unloose: He shall baptize you with the Holy Ghost and with fire...

Helper
John 14:15-16
[15] If you love Me, keep My commandments.

[16] And I will pray the Father, and he shall give you another Comforter, that he may abide with you for ever...

It is by Him, our Helper, that we are able to live by and do what is right.

Living Water
John 7:38-39

[38] He that believeth on Me, as the Scripture hath said, out of his belly shall flow rivers of living water.

[39] (But this spake He of the Spirit, which they that believe on Him should receive: for the Holy Ghost was not yet given; because that Jesus was not yet glorified.)

Power
Luke 24:49

And, behold, I send the promise of my Father upon you: but tarry ye in the city of Jerusalem, until ye be endued with power from on high.

Acts 1:8

But ye shall receive power, after that the Holy Ghost is come upon you: and ye shall be witnesses unto Me both in Jerusalem, and in all Judaea, and in Samaria, and unto the uttermost part of the earth.

Teacher
John 14:26

But the Comforter, which is the Holy Ghost, whom the Father will send in My name, He shall teach you all things, and bring all things to your remembrance, whatsoever I have said unto you.

Spirit of Adoption
Romans 8:15

For ye have not received the spirit of bondage again to fear; but ye have received the Spirit of Adoption, whereby we cry, Abba, Father.

Spirit of God
Romans 8:14

For as many as are led by the Spirit of God, they are the sons of God.

Spirit of Life
Romans 8:2

For the law of the Spirit of life in Christ Jesus hath made me free from the law of sin and death.

Spirit of Truth
John 14:16-17

[16] And I will pray the Father, and He shall give you another Comforter, that He may abide with you for ever;

[17] Even the Spirit of truth; whom the world cannot receive, because it seeth Him not, neither knoweth Him: but ye know Him; for He dwelleth with you, and shall be in you.

There is no complexity intended in knowing the characteristics of the Holy Spirit. In understanding them, all uncertainty and helplessness lose their effectiveness against us because our Help is here and we know it. We have taken hold of all our Help contains. By the evidence we have in the Names of the Holy Spirit we are assured, and can be confident of and in our Father's promise to never leave, fail or forsake us…we are never alone.

CHAPTER VII

OUR HEAVENLY
PRAYER LANGUAGE

<u>OUR HEAVENLY PRAYER LANGUAGE</u>

Acts 2:1-4
[1] And when the day of Pentecost was fully come, they were all
with one accord in one place.

[2] And suddenly there came a sound from heaven as of a rushing
mighty wind, and it filled all the house where they were sitting.

[3] And there appeared unto them cloven tongues like as of fire,
and it sat upon each of them.

[4] And they were all filled with the Holy Ghost, and began to
speak with other tongues, as the Spirit gave them utterance.

One of the evidences of being baptized in the Holy Ghost is the
utterance or speaking in other tongues. It is your own personal
heavenly prayer language. Praying in the Spirit is speaking in an
unknown tongue, that is, speaking in a tongue or language that
is unknown to the intellect. The devil cannot decipher it and
your flesh cannot alter it. It is a divine language between the
Lord and you; untainted by your experiences, emotions and
observations.

Romans 8:26-27
[26] Likewise the Spirit also helpeth our infirmities: for we know
not what we should pray for as we ought: but the Spirit itself

maketh intercession for us with groanings which cannot be uttered.

27 And He that searcheth the hearts knoweth what is the mind of the Spirit, because He maketh intercession for the saints according to the will of God.

In praying in the Spirit you are actually praying the heart, the will of God. It is the pure, unadulterated language of heaven. Every New Creature in Christ has his/her personal dialect with Him. Oftentimes as I am praying, especially when called to intercede *(pray for others)*, my speaking may flow into what will sound different as of another heavenly dialect; but it is still divine – of God.

There are times when the Lord may instruct me to call out names and then pray in the Spirit only. In this I am praying His perfect will for them. Sometimes it may alternate between a heavenly language and earthly, known language.

Sometimes when praying in the Spirit it may sound as another known language but foreign to the person speaking – for example it may have an Asian lilt to it or Middle Eastern or African or European when the person's known language is English. This reminds me of Acts 2:7-8 when they all heard the message in their own language although those speaking were from Galilee.

I have heard some argue that this alone is what is meant by, "praying in an unknown tongue." This does occur just as in the account given in Acts, for the Lord promises to make His heart known to all His children; and He will do so in the way that accomplishes His will and glorify Him. However, there is more.

1 Corinthians 14:2, 4

² For he that speaketh in an unknown tongue speaketh not unto men, but unto God: for no man understandeth him; howbeit in the spirit he speaketh mysteries.

⁴ He that speaketh in an unknown tongue edifieth himself; but he that prophesieth edifieth the church.

This statement of Scripture provides proof that there is more. According to these verses "speaking in an unknown tongue" is not speaking to men; no man understands...men cannot comprehend what is spoken. Therefore, based on these verses, there must be more than merely speaking in another known language from a foreign land; for that alone would not cause the edifying mentioned here.

Praying in an "unknown tongue" or "in the Spirit" is praying what is a mystery to the natural man or intellect. It is available to <u>every</u> believer, is activated when accepting and receiving the baptism of the Holy Spirit, and is spoken to communicate directly with the Lord Himself. He will provide the interpretation, especially when spoken in a crowd-type setting, congregation or public worship. We are even encouraged to ask the Lord for the ability to interpret.

1 Corinthians 14:13-14

¹³ Wherefore let him that speaketh in and unknown tongue pray that he may interpret.

¹⁴ For if I pray in an unknown tongue, my spirit prayeth, but my understanding is unfruitful.

There are those who doubt there is speaking in tongues, or believe that praying in the Spirit is not Biblical. But the apostle Paul admits he himself spoke a heavenly language.

1 Corinthians 14:15, 18

¹⁵ What is it then? I will pray with the spirit, and I will pray with the understanding also: I will sing with the spirit, and I will sing with the understanding also.

¹⁸ I thank my God, I speak with tongues more than you all

There are still others who wonder if it is necessary, beneficial or relevant. But I, like Paul, am grateful for the ability to pray and sing in the Spirit, in heavenly tongues. When I do not know what to pray, I pray in the Spirit, communicating with the Lord Himself on the matter, and I know I speak His answer as He reveals it.

Testimony:
I had just become a lay-minister at the church I was attending at the time and praying for people at the altar was new to and for me. A woman came forward asking me to pray for healing. As she was speaking I was moved to mutter (softly pray in the Spirit) to myself. I remember thinking that I would not be able to hear what she was saying. Then the Holy Spirit, lovingly impressed on my heart that it did not matter that I could not hear her, for I was speaking to the One who had and would provide the answer; to which my heart responded with an, "Oh, that's right...oops."

When she finished describing the ailment, pain and how the doctor was unable to determine a prognosis I began to pray for her. I kept trying to pray in English for healing based on what she had asked but it was as if I was tongue-tied. I kept stumbling over the words. Then I began praying in the Spirit, and the understanding, by interpretation, came. I received revelation that the issue was not the need for physical healing but for her to relinquish control to God. He revealed that she was spreading herself so thin, carrying the burdens of others, which she was not meant to carry; and led me to instruct her to submit all to Him.

Upon completing the prayer, I feebly asked her if she was alright. I was unsure because, in the natural I "knew" that was not the prayer she requested – I told you this was new to me at that time. She was a bit annoyed and said that it was okay; that was not what she wanted; but she would just take what she could from it. I felt as though the wind was let out of my sails, thinking I had failed God and this woman. I could not get to my car fast enough to cry my apologies to the Lord. He revealed that I had done well and spoken correctly. He filled me with His amazing peace.

A few weeks later she excitedly stopped me in the hall at church to tell me she had been looking for me to report that she had returned to the doctor, nothing physical could be found, and the diagnosis was stress. Then she thanked me. I immediately responded, "Thank You, Jesus," for it definitely was not of my own doing.

The pure language of heaven can also be appreciated during worship. On many occasions, when I am blessing the Lord in worship – reflecting on His awesomeness; speaking of His goodness; thanking Him for His faithfulness; honoring El-Elyon, the Most High God – it will get so intense as my heart becomes full with desire to convey my love and adoration to Him that I find there are no earthly words adequate enough and am compelled to continue in my heavenly tongue. It is at these times I am grateful for my prayer language, which enables me to more aptly articulate what is in my heart for my God.

Our prayer language may also be expressed in song. There are times when God's peace and comfort will fill the room or overtake a situation in the soothing melody of singing in the Spirit.

Testimony:
My son was in the hospital for emergency surgery. When he had come out of recovery and was moved to his room we busied ourselves with getting him settled, and come to terms with what had just occurred. At my attempt to ease his heart as mothers do, the Holy Spirit moved on mine to begin singing a worship song from church. As I sang, all our hearts began to calm, moving out the fear and tension that had mistakenly thought they could set up camp.

The Spirit of God inspired me to instinctively – as first nature – worship the Lord; it rose up out of my spirit. I started in English, then the Holy Spirit took over, changing it over to a divine tongue. The melody was the same, but the language had been elevated. Then an exquisite presence of God filled the room, peace that passes all understanding overtook us all. It was wonderful and so very needed by everyone in that room.

I had not fully realized the power of that moment until someone relayed to me my oldest son's account of it. Glory to God!

James 1:17
Every good gift and every perfect gift is from above, and cometh down from the Father of lights, with whom is no variableness, neither shadow of turning.

The Father has not changed His mind, retracting His gifts. What He gave then He gives now for us to enjoy, appreciate and utilize in service and worship. Although the natural man struggles to understand, and the devil fights to keep us ignorant of its merits, I implore you to accept this gift of God; if for no other initial reason but to acquire everything God has for you. Then allow the Holy Spirit to work things out from there.

REFLECTIONS

The Holy Spirit is oftentimes limited in consideration to being merely a benefit of Salvation. It is true that Salvation precedes receiving the Holy Spirit; however, He is a Person of the Godhead, with the same power, anointing and magnitude of the Father and the Son. Therefore, we must take the time to know, respect and appreciate Him for who and all He is.

When first beginning to speak in your heavenly language, you may feel awkward, self-conscious and unsure. Think of the small child beginning to speak, uttering sounds and eventually forming words...sentences... phrases, etc.; so it is with you child of God. As you persist you will notice that it will become more fluent and you will converse with God in ease; and in the interim know that your Father God understands every sound. Just continue to flow in and with the Holy Spirit.

SECTION FIVE

THE PRESENCE OF GOD

FOUNDATION SCRIPTURES:
Psalm 46:10
Be still, and know that I am God: I will be exalted among the heathen, I will be exalted in the earth.

1 Kings 8:56
Blessed be the LORD, that hath given rest unto his people Israel, according to all that he promised: there hath not failed one word of all his good promise, which he promised by the hand of Moses his servant.

INTRODUCTION
The Lord gives rest to His people just as He has promised. This rest comes in our confidence in His faithfulness – not one word of His promises shall or even can fail.

The "rest" spoken of in this foundation text is translated from Hebrew words meaning repose, peacefully, abode, comfortable, quiet, resting place; still, a settled spot, a home; to settle down, dwell, let fall, place, let alone, withdraw, give comfort, cause to...to be at...to give/have/make to rest, set down.

We are to rest, settle down and be at peace – this is God's design. It is His Sabbath rest, accomplished and fully realized by our practicing the presence of God. Opening our hearts to getting acquainted with the Godhead enables us to settle into His presence as a lifestyle – He becomes our settled spot, that place to dwell and from which we are to operate. It is where we can be real, allowing ourselves the vulnerability of nakedness before Him; while feeling safe, covered and protected in His glory and love.

CHAPTER I

IN THE PRESENCE OF GOD

IN THE PRESENCE OF GOD

Practicing the presence of God is achieved by His Holy Spirit. By the Names of the Holy Spirit we come to know His characteristics and are thereby "provided" the depth and magnitude of God's continually saying, "I am with you, whithersoever *(wherever)* you go;" and Jesus' stating, "...lo, I am with you alway." *(Joshua 1:9; Matthew 28:20)*

This practicing is not as in "keep trying until you get it and then you are done", but rather of doing it, walking it, living it.

John 1:1-5
¹ In the beginning was the Word, and the Word was with God, and the Word was God.

² The same was in the beginning with God.

³ All things were made by him; and without him was not any thing made that was made.

⁴ In him was life; and the life was the light of men.

⁵ And the light shineth in darkness; and the darkness comprehended it not.

The world is very much geared toward "self" – doing things your own way, being free to live. Well real living, to the degree God has intended, does not and cannot occur apart from God. It is

His desire and plan that we abide in each other – we in Him and He in us, by His Holy Spirit.

Genesis 5:21-24
[21] And Enoch lived sixty and five years, and begat Methuselah:

[22] And Enoch walked with God after he begat Methuselah three hundred years, and begat sons and daughters:

[23] And all the days of Enoch were three hundred sixty and five years:

[24] And Enoch walked with God: and he *was* not; for God took him.

(Notice how Enoch, who walked so closely with God, did not actually begin until he was sixty-five years old. It is never too late. Start where you are.)

Hebrews 11:5
By faith Enoch was translated that he should not see death; and was not found, because God had translated him: for before his translation he had this testimony, that he pleased God.

We please God when we abide and walk with Him.

Initially, when I heard about walking with the Lord, I thought, "This is cool…walk with God, wow." Then reasoning filtered in and I thought, "Walk with Almighty God – how do you do that?"

- It is in fellowship with Him – reading and meditating on Him by His Word, praise, worship, thanksgiving, fasting, prayer and being still.

- It is in intimacy with Him – practicing…living the presence of Him.

This is how we hear Him – counsel *(instruction and direction)*, encouragement, jokes *(He has a wonderful sense of humor)*. We experience His love, affection and care when we abide in Him.

Isaiah 30:21
And thine ears shall hear a word behind thee, saying, This is the way, walk ye in it, when ye turn to the right hand, and when ye turn to the left.

Testimony

I purchased a book at 50% off; a Christian historical novel to read for some rest and relaxation time, not realizing it was part of a series, which is not my favorite thing because of time constraints and continuity. As it turned out, I really enjoyed it. At completing it, I went to the store for something else and happened to find the second book of the series for 75% off. After some searching, I could only find the third and final book online, which happened to only be at 12-13% off. Each time I attempted to purchase it, that still small voice of the Holy Spirit, would say, "Wait." He was even patient at my excitement at finding it and attempts to reason His permission from Him, but I waited. Then one day, I "came across" it in a store, marked 50% off and He gave the release to get it. At the register, it rang up for 97¢; at 96% off.

As for continuity, the plot and all the characters were as fresh to me as though no time had passed at all between readings.

Religion tells us that we should not or that we do not have to bother God with every little thing; that there is no need to seek Him for the mundane. But that is so contrary to His plan of fellowship with us. He is not a fireman, only there to help in emergencies. Relationship tells us that He desires to be involved in everything concerning us – the good, bad, big, small, happy and sad times...everything. This is fellowship; this is intimacy.

Deuteronomy 5:33
Ye shall walk in all the ways which the LORD your God hath commanded you, that ye may live, and that it may be well with you, and that ye may prolong your days in the land which ye shall possess.

Jeremiah 7:23
But this thing commanded I them, saying, Obey my voice, and I will be your God, and ye shall be my people: and walk ye in all the ways that I have commanded you, that it may be well unto you.

Isaiah 48:17
Thus saith the LORD, thy Redeemer, the Holy One of Israel; I am the LORD thy God which teacheth thee to profit, which leadeth thee by the way that thou shouldest go.

For all this to come to be we must hear and obey God – this is a must; but we must also be intimate with Him. The devil has perverted intimacy to be a matter of lust; but the Lord has ordained it...it is of Love.

Just so we are all on the same page, with the same understanding in this: intimacy requires some quiet and stillness. Our being in, but not of, a world that is constantly going and moving, our being quiet will take some exercise. Keep at it until you achieve stillness in and of His presence; until it becomes your practice *(lifestyle)*. This by no means is a slothful *(lazy)* way of living. Remember the Lord teaches us to profit and leads us in the way we are to go – there is action and activity in that.

CHAPTER II

PRACTICING (LIVING) THE PRESENCE OF GOD

PRACTICING (LIVING) THE PRESENCE OF GOD

It is in worship that we live in Him in the manner He so desires and has arranged – worship in and by our lifestyle:

1. Obeying Him – following His instruction

2. Being still – taking the time-outs on your own volition – you making the time to honor and fellowship with Him

3. Make lifestyle fellowship statements to Him:
    a. Say good morning when you arise – "Good morning Father...Good morning Jesus...Good morning Holy Spirit."
    b. Say thank You and good night when you turn in; acknowledge Him and His existence in your life

4. Ask Him lifestyle fellowship questions:
    a. Lord, what is on Our agenda today?
    b. Where shall We go to eat today?
    c. What name shall I call my child/business – what name have You chosen?
    d. Where is Our new home? Take me to Our new home.

5. Express your admiration and affection to Him – "Lord, I just want to praise You right now; not asking for anything – only loving and appreciating You."

I personally use music a great deal. Appreciating the beauty of His creations and His creativity will also "still" me and suspend the noise around me.   Focus on Him unto stillness, peace, appreciation and worship.

CHAPTER III

APPLICATION

Psalm 46:10
Be still, and know that I am God: I will be exalted among the heathen, I will be exalted in the earth.

Living the presence of God requires being still, quieting yourself to hear His reassurances, to receive showers of His love, to allow Him to wrap you in His blanket of peace, and to clearly see visions of the plans He has established for you. In these "be still" sessions, which I have heard some refer to as "soaking," word(s) and/or images may be given *(revealed)* to you; or it may be that you are to experience the warmth of His compassion at that particular sitting. The hearing may be as a thought or the still small voice of Him. The Lord is very creative. Think about it: how special would special be if it came the same way all the time? He desires our intimacy with Him to be special.

There are various ways of practice to enter into the "be still":

1. The Bible
Incorporate the Word of God to set the atmosphere. Read verses of pure worship unto God that describe His awesomeness; then lead into prayer of worship and appreciation.
Here is an example to get you started:
    a. Read Revelation 4:8-11, 5:11-14
    b. Immediately follow with expressions of adoration to Him
    c. Write what He says to you *(impresses on your heart)*

2. Music

Music can set the atmosphere of the room, and the personal atmosphere of your heart in shifting your focus fully onto Him. As the music plays listen for Him. It may be one word or many, but write what you hear.

    a. Play music – uplifting, reflective, goodness-of-God-focused assortments. Include some instrumental selections.

    b. Listen for Him

    c. Write what He puts on your heart

3. Prayer

Praying in the Spirit, your heavenly tongue *(language)*, will override your emotions and thoughts.

    a. Pray in the Spirit

    b. Stop and listen

    c. Write what you hear and descriptions of any visions He may present to you

4. Quiet – Be Still

You may need to incorporate some of the other examples to adjust your focus to conquer the noise vying for your attention to fully appreciate this practice.

    a. Play a worship song; pray or sing in the Spirit

    b. Be quiet – just listen...close your eyes and listen

    c. Write what He reveals

Praise and thank Him for His attention and affection for you. Live in expectation of and appreciation for His love, care and compassion. These examples are given to usher you into a lifestyle of listening for and recognizing His voice. As you continue, you shall discover and develop in Him other methods of nearness.

<u>REFLECTIONS</u>

To sit still, listen and actually hear God speak, or to see His plans for you may all seem far-fetched. But as you become more acquainted with Him and make abiding in Him a practice, you will discover the very real possibility of living this way. As you continue, your heart will desire more and more of Him; and the Holy Spirit is more than happy to oblige.

SALVATION BENEFITS – THE BLESSING OF THE LORD

<u>SALVATION BENEFITS – THE BLESSING OF THE LORD</u>

<u>FOUNDATION SCRIPTURES:</u>
3 John 2
Beloved, I wish above all things that thou mayest prosper and be in health, even as thy soul prospereth.

Psalm 24:5
He shall receive the blessing from the LORD, and righteousness from the God of his salvation.

Psalm 68:19
Blessed *be* the Lord, *who* daily loadeth us *with benefits, even* the God of our salvation. Selah.

INTRODUCTION

It is the will of the Father for His children to be healthy, wealthy and whole. Wealth is much more expansive than the material. Consider "shalom," the Hebrew word translated to English is "peace." However, this word "peace" encompasses peace, health, favor and prosperity. And so it is with "wealth," which addresses our entire well-being: mind, body and soul; spiritual and natural; and yes, material also.

The blessing of the Lord is the Salvation benefit afforded to us by God personally. In His divine and perfectly executed plan, God has ensured that we have everything we need to live victoriously right here, now, in this life in wholeness.

2 Peter 1:3
According as his divine power hath given unto us all things that pertain unto life and godliness, through the knowledge of him that hath called us to glory and virtue:

Mark 10:30
But he shall receive an hundredfold now in this time, houses, and brethren, and sisters, and mothers, and children, and lands, with persecutions; and in the world to come eternal life.

Numbers 23:19
God is not a man, that he should lie; neither the son of man, that he should repent: hath he said, and shall he not do it? or hath he spoken, and shall he not make it good?

There are many benefits associated with Salvation that are oftentimes taken for granted or not recognized as rightfully ours through the perfect work of Jesus Christ. Healing, deliverance, prosperity, peace, joy, love and compassion for others, strength and boldness are all included. These and much more are associated with the blessing of the Lord, given unto us at the time of Salvation.

God is not in the business of making empty promises to us; there are no vain babblings with Him. He actually watches to ensure they are fulfilled. He, all-power *(omnipotent)*, all-knowing *(omniscient)* and all-present *(omnipresent)*, has what it takes to cause it all to manifest according to His will.

CHAPTER I

IMPLEMENTATION

IMPLEMENTATION

God has completed His work concerning us. He has established the blessing we are to receive and our purpose in Him. His work is done and all ready for us to possess and implement. There are steps of implementation for us to observe and follow.

1. Abiding
Psalm 91:1
He that dwelleth in the secret place of the most High shall abide under the shadow of the Almighty.

John 15:7
If ye abide in me, and my words abide in you, ye shall ask what ye will, and it shall be done unto you.

Abiding is getting acquainted with Him to know who He is and then who we are in Him; becoming intimate with Him; and getting into "that place" in Him. The benefits are realized in the abiding.

2. Renewing the mind
Romans 12:2
And be not conformed to this world: but be ye transformed by the renewing of your mind, that ye may prove what *is* that good, and acceptable, and perfect, will of God.

Salvation immediately transforms our spirit man; however, to enjoy the fullness of God and His blessing, and live a victorious life there must be a renewing of the mind:

a. To shift thoughts, responses and perspective from that of the world to that of the Kingdom of God.

b. To understand our place and function as representatives of God and His Kingdom here in the earth

c. To discover how to utilize the benefits He has made available to us

d. To shift confidence from the world and its system to God and His Kingdom's system

3. Character building

2 Peter 1:3-8

[3] According as his divine power hath given unto us all things that pertain unto life and godliness, through the knowledge of him that hath called us to glory and virtue:

[4] Whereby are given unto us exceeding great and precious promises: that by these ye might be partakers of the divine nature, having escaped the corruption that is in the world through lust.

[5] And beside this, giving all diligence, add to your faith virtue; and to virtue knowledge;

[6] And to knowledge temperance; and to temperance patience; and to patience godliness;

[7] And to godliness brotherly kindness; and to brotherly kindness charity.

[8] For if these things be in you, and abound, they make you that ye shall neither be barren nor unfruitful in the knowledge of our Lord Jesus Christ.

Changing systems and determining to totally go and operate the Kingdom of God way will require your character to be checked, renewed, built, and overhauled in and by God. By this we can step out in faith, stand boldly, maintain Godly integrity, persevere, and impact the earth for expansion of the Kingdom and the glory of God.

The perpetual observance of these steps helps us to maintain the initial and ongoing work of the Holy Spirit to perfect us. We are to check ourselves; go to God asking Him to reveal any breach when we perceive something is not quite right, or feel that something is amiss; and follow through as He instructs. When we comply with His course of implementation, which may include one process *(or many)*, of wait, of preparation, of wilderness and of being alone *(not lonely)*:

We learn to...
> Trust in the LORD with all thine heart; and lean not unto thine own understanding. *(Proverbs 3:5)*

We become...
> And he shall be like a tree planted by the rivers of water, that bringeth forth his fruit in his season; his leaf also shall not wither; and whatsoever he doeth shall prosper. *(Psalm 1:3)*

We determine...
> I can do all things through Christ which strengtheneth me. *(Philippians 4:13)*

We know...
> But my God shall supply all your need according to his riches in glory by Christ Jesus. *(Philippians 4:19)*

...all because we understand 1 John 5:4-5
> [4] For whatsoever is born of God overcometh the world: and this is the victory that overcometh the world, even our faith.

> [5] Who is he that overcometh the world, but he that believeth that Jesus is the Son of God?

CHAPTER II

RESPONSIBILITY

<u>RESPONSIBILITY</u>

Esther 4:13-14

[13] Then Mordecai commanded to answer Esther, Think not with thyself that thou shalt escape in the king's house, more than all the Jews.

[14] For if thou altogether holdest thy peace at this time, then shall there enlargement and deliverance arise to the Jews from another place; but thou and thy father's house shall be destroyed: and who knoweth whether thou art come to the kingdom for such a time as this?

With all this revelation comes the awareness that we cannot keep it all to ourselves. The more time we spend with the Lord the more intense our love for Him becomes, and we reach a place where we desire others to experience this phenomenal love as well. This desire coupled with wisdom we receive from God makes our witness of Him to others most effective through our testimony, which is first our lifestyle and then our conversation. We are presentations of God's handiwork and faithfulness, as people come to know He really does save, deliver, heal, provide, protect...bless, as they witness Him in us.

With the blessing comes responsibility. Jesus Himself tells us that He has given us power to tread on serpents and scorpions and nothing shall by any means harm us. *(Luke 10:19)* This is not for show, for our enjoyment, or just for those in our immediate circle. We are blessed, equipped and anointed to do the work of the Kingdom of God. Yes, we are to enjoy the abundant life as God has promised and provides, but that is not the end of it.

We are blessed to be a blessing to those He sends us. We are ambassadors of the Kingdom of God, extensions of Him in the earth; to implement His will here. So we are to go and impart, teach, share His love and what He has given us as He leads, resulting from our intimate fellowship with Him. But even in all this, the greatest benefit of our Salvation is the ability to be with the Father personally and confidently, in camaraderie. This truly supersedes anything else.

REFLECTIONS

Oh, what an awesome thing it is to abide in the Lord and He abiding in us; to truly become One with the Almighty. This is how we enter into His rest, abiding there; in the place where the devil cannot affect us. This is our wealthy place. Join the many others who cry out Abba, Father – Daddy, God. Live Him and share Him. Enjoy your heavenly Father; enjoy the nearness of Him.
Amen.

SECTION SEVEN

PRAYER OF SALVATION AND BAPTISM IN THE HOLY SPIRIT

<u>PRAYER OF SALVATION AND BAPTISM IN THE HOLY SPIRIT</u>

<u>FOUNDATION SCRIPTURE:</u>
Romans 10:9-10
⁹ That if thou shalt confess with thy mouth the Lord Jesus, and shalt believe in thine heart that God hath raised Him from the dead, thou shalt be saved.

¹⁰ For with the heart man believeth unto righteousness; and with the mouth confession is made unto salvation.

<u>INTRODUCTION</u>
It is the will of the Father...His heart's desire that no one would perish. Jesus even tells us of how a shepherd will leave the ninety-nine sheep to go after the one that has gone astray...and so does our Good Shepherd: pursuing and wooing us. He came so none would perish...He came for us...He came for you. Even

155

when in the thick of some mess, He was still calling us unto Himself. What an awesome God. What a beautiful Savior.

If you would like to accept and confess Jesus Christ, making Him your personal Lord and Savior *or* if you have turned away from Him to go your own way and wish to return to Him, make your confession by praying the following prayer aloud for Salvation and to receive the gift of the Holy Spirit.

<u>PRAYER</u>

Dear Jesus,
I believe You are the Son of God.

I believe You died and rose from the dead on the third day.

I believe You are alive and seated at the right hand of the Father.

I believe You died for my sin; paying the debt for sin that I could never pay myself.

Please forgive me for all my sin. Please come into my heart and be the Lord over my life.

I confess right now that You are my Lord and Savior as I have asked, received and accepted.

I am forgiven. I am now born-again. I am now a child of God.
Thank You, Lord.

Now I ask You for the gift of the Holy Spirit, filling me with power from on high. I expect to speak in other tongues and I thank You for my heavenly prayer language.

Thank You for it all Father, in the Name of Jesus Christ.
Amen.

If you have just made Jesus the Lord of your life, know that all of heaven is celebrating right now. Hallelujah! Glory to God!

Begin reading your Bible daily to enhance your intimacy with the Godhead. Be sure to regularly attend a church that boldly teaches the complete Word of God and lives It. Become part of your church family; partake of the opportunities to learn more about the Father; ask Him in which activities and ministries He desires you to serve; and connect with other members of the body of Christ of which you are now a part.

Congratulations and Welcome to the Family!
Many blessings to you.

Reference Scriptures:
Matthew 18:11-14; Luke 15:10; John 3:16; Acts 8:37;
Romans 3:23-25, 6:23, 10:9-10; Romans 14:9; 2 Corinthians 5:17;
Hebrews 10:25

END NOTES

[1] Webster's New World Dictionary, Fourth Edition © 2000 by IDG Books Worldwide, Inc.

[2] Dictionary.com. Collins English Dictionary – Complete and Unabridged 10th Edition. HarperCollins Publishers (accessed Oct. 9, 2013)

[3] Strong's Hebrew and Greek Dictionaries – e-Sword Version 10.1.0 © 2000-2012 Rick Meyers

[4] Brown-Driver-Briggs Hebrew and English Lexicon, Unabridged, Electronic Database Copyright © 2002, 2003, 2006 by Biblesoft, Inc.

MEET THE AUTHOR

 Tedi H. Marshall began her service to the Lord as an usher at New Life Celebration Church of God, Dolton, IL; the Lord then making room for her gift in the role of Lay Minister, specializing in Pastoral Care, and in the Intercessory Prayer Ministry. She advanced to Chaplain for the Lay Ministers and Ministers; supporting through prayer, encouragement and organizing and conducting special services; and eventually becoming Chaplain to the Pastors. She is currently a Pastoral Care and Altar Minister at Living Word Christian Center, Forest Park, IL.

Pastor Tedi graduated from The School of Ministry in Forest Park, IL and is also a graduate of New Life Institute in Dolton, IL, where she followed the ministerial tract of study. She has taught at New Life Institute and teaches at Living Word Bible Training Center; and assisted in research for the development of cell group ministry at Living Word Christian Center. She has served on the ministerial staff at New Life Celebration Church of God and was licensed within the Church of God denomination in the rank of Exhorter.

Some of her ministry assignments have included preaching/teaching the Word of God at Living Word Christian Center, New Life Celebration Church of God, and City of Hope Church of God in Chicago, IL, and various other church services; teaching classes and various Bible studies, conferences, and workshops; assisting in the planting of a new church in roles of usher, treasury, minister, and in the Intercessory Prayer and Women's Ministries.

She is Founder and Pastor of WORD Fellowship Ministries, equipping others to lead and assist with establishing and facilitating small group Bible studies and intercessory prayer sessions; and outreach assignments in partnership with other ministries. She issues weekly online newsletters featuring devotion messages and testimonies submitted of God's handiwork, and a blog of prophetic messages; conducts spiritual guidance sessions based on the Bible; makes pastoral care calls and visits as the Lord leads; all to glorify God in word and deed.

Having worked in the Accounting field most of her adult life, the Holy Spirit called her into a new career as business owner of My Prayer, Inc. Pastor Tedi has dedicated her life as a minister, artist and published author to sharing the love of God wherever He sends her.

Her charge is to preach, teach, prophesy, exhort, counsel, and war in the heavenlies through prayer, praise, and worship; and edify others to walk in the liberty and benefits provided by Jesus Christ.

She has received several awards, certificates and recognition in non-secular and secular arenas alike.

If this book has impacted your life, please share your testimony. Email Pastor Tedi Marshall to share your testimony or schedule an appearance at marshall.tedi@gmail.com

Made in the USA
Monee, IL
28 April 2023

32626012R00100